MEDITATION

for

DAILY STRESS

MEDITATION

for

DAILY STRESS

10

Practices

for

Immediate

Well-being

Michel Pascal

Abrams Image, New York

Contents

Foreword

Meditation for Daily Stress is the beginning of a revolution in the
world of meditation, with profound implications for the world
of medicine. To meditate for any amount of time is valuable, but
Michel Pascal has created a new way to be mindful, one that
requires only a minute of your time. He proves that this is all the
time you need to receive the benefits of meditation and makes it
incredibly easy to adopt these practices throughout the day and
throughout the week.

Michel's meditation techniques activate regions of the brain
involved in intention and attention that can inhibit activity in the
amygdala, the older, more primitive region of the limbic system
that can trigger our fight or flight, or acute stress, response. As
you begin meditation, your breath becomes relaxed—slow and
full. This positive change in your breathing is incredibly important
for regulating the sympathetic nervous system and the relaxation
response. Healthy breathing allows our tissues and organs to

receive more oxygen-rich blood, necessary for the healthy functioning of all of our cells, tissues, and organs.

The chemical response to stress is cortisol, released from our adrenal gland. It increases blood pressure, heart rate, and muscle tension. Importantly, cortisol decreases our immune function and suppresses the activity of important immunoglobulins, cytokines, and natural killer cells. Cortisol is beneficial when we need to increase blood flow to our muscles in threatening situations, such as an attack by a mugger, but when activated in nonthreatening situations, such as through repetitive stressful thoughts, increased cortisol can be severely detrimental to our health. Stress negatively contributes to nearly all illness and disease, and Michel's short, accessible meditation practices, with their positive visualizations, can act as a preventative measure against poor health.

The best part of the relaxation response elicited by a brief meditation session is inherently rewarding—it feels good! This means the meditation is activating what is called the dopaminergic reward pathway, the brain pathways involved in experiencing pleasure. These pathways and the function of dopamine and other neurotransmitters within them are involved in the pleasurable feelings that accompany love, food, sex, and some drugs. Meditation allows us to naturally increase the functioning of these pathways without resorting to unhealthy behaviors, such as drug abuse or high sugar and fat intake.

The practice of meditation can also shine a spotlight on any hidden and destructive thoughts we may have. When we learn to better control our thoughts through daily meditation, we are able to transcend aspects of our ego that cause suffering. With just a short meditation session you will notice more and be more engaged in your life experience. Meditation also allows us to tap into higher states of consciousness, characterized by an expanded sense of awareness and unity, a non-dual state of loving–kindness. Even brief meditation sessions, like the practices recommended in this book, can profoundly reduce stress, improve immune function, increase positive emotions, and allow for personal and spiritual transformation.

—Natalie L. Trent, PhD, Harvard University

Preface: The Discipline of Happiness

Discovering neuroscience was a revelation to me. It taught me that we are not the slaves of our past. We have the capacity to change every day, every minute, to reproduce new neurons until our last day. We don't have to possess bad character; we are not our traumas. We are not our past. We are not our mental habits. We can change now, immediately. This is not wishful thinking or fantasy. It is the reality of human neuroplasticity—our ability to alter our brain's neural synapses and pathways—and it is achievable through the practice of meditation.

Our brain is a muscle, and every day is a chance to develop the brain. We can further build and enhance our character, our determination, our happiness, our intuition, and our freedom.

Yes, we really can do this! We can become more present, more intelligent, more compassionate, and much more free. Right now. The goal of meditation is to live a freer, clearer, and happier life. One day, a novice asked Saint Therese of Lisieux, "What is faith?" Therese replied, "Faith is happiness, because everything is a blessing and a grace."

To train your mind and to meditate can become the ultimate revelation of your life. Yes, you can! Yes, it is possible! Everyday when I see my students, and when I see the people I am working with at the Amity Foundation—a community rehabilitation center in Los Angeles that is dedicated to the inclusion and habilitation of prisoners, parolees, children, and families marginalized by homelessness, poverty, addiction, crime, racism, sexism, trauma, and violence—it makes me cry. I see how simple it is, in reality, to make a difference.

What do we need to improve our lives? Determination and discipline. Why is it so difficult to meditate? There are two primary reasons:

1. Our false perception of meditation. The cliché of the monk who meditates for many hours in his shrine or on a mountaintop has encouraged a false perception of the practice. This standard image has made meditation seem unachievable, because our daily lives are not in sync with the fantasy.

We must learn that to meditate and to train our minds is possible in just a few minutes per day, anytime, and anywhere. We must see how every situation in our life is an occasion to train our determination.

2. Our false perception of discipline. We have been taught that the practice of discipline is like an effort against ourselves. Think about the quest of losing weight. We know it is possible, but to make the effort and be disciplined is too difficult, especially in the midst of our daily stress. How can we find the energy to meditate when we have no energy left just to live our lives? How is discipline possible when we are very busy and overbooked every day? Why must discipline be sad, strict, and negative?

Discipline means freedom. Every day, we can take a few minutes to feel better. We develop a near chemical addiction to happiness, peace, and a quiet mind.

We need only a few minutes to meditate every day. The most important goal here is not the quantity but the quality of the practice. In just one minute, we have the ability to touch our soul and the spiritual dimension. We can be connected to the eternity of the universe in a very short amount of time. We must prioritize the quality of our meditation practice over the duration of it. Every situation is a wonderful occasion to meditate, to feel at peace immediately.

> Every time we wake up in bed is an opportunity.
> Every coffee we have is an opportunity.
> Every moment in traffic is an opportunity.
> Every moment we are in the subway, on a train, or riding
>   the bus is an opportunity.
> Every time we arrive at our workplace is an opportunity.

Life is like a movie; there is a start and an end. After each new movie, each new moment is a new reincarnation. Life keeps going on. Most of the time, we are the actors in our life movie.

We are directed by our emotions and our mental habits. To practice meditation opens the mind to another perception of consciousness. Day after day, we become less the actor and more the director. When we practice and we train our minds, suddenly one day we will be out of the movie, out of the set, and out of the screen. We will find ourselves sitting down at the front row of our theater.

We will have a different perception of our movie. We will see our emotions as a director sees his actors. By then, we can say to an actor, "I don't like how you act. I won't keep you in my cast." We can say the same thing for our emotions. For example, when we see that we are anxious and we don't like it, we can say, "I'm sorry dear anxious emotion, dear actor, I am canceling your contract. You are no longer in my movie. Get out!"

The goal of meditation is not to become more spiritual or religious. It is to become more present, calmer, happier, and freer. These are the goals of this life, after all.

Introduction

Stress may be the greatest epidemic of our time.

I am no stranger to the troubling consequences of stress. My father, an entrepreneur who sadly lost his business, died before my eyes from a heart attack, panicked and distressed by financial troubles.

When I met my assistant, her health was completely destroyed by stress. As an employee of a large corporation in New York City, day in and day out she pushed herself to complete amounts of work that were clearly not suitable for just one employee. With about ten minutes to eat lunch every day, she was surrounded by coworkers drowning in stress of their own. She had no sense of peace in her daily life. Her mind was running all the time; she would leave her office, but the anxiety, worry, and stress from her job consumed her well-being. She, and everyone around her, truly believed high levels of stress were just part of the job— the norm.

One day while crossing the street after work, she collapsed

in the middle of oncoming traffic. Concerned, she went to the doctor. She completed blood work, an MRI and a CAT scan, a cardiac CT scan—a full physical examination. The doctors could not find one thing wrong with her health. The problem was debilitating stress.

Unfortunately, her case is becoming common, especially in big cities. Adrenal and thyroid complications, chronic migraines, insomnia, depression, and chronic fatigue are plaguing people of all ages, and often the true culprit goes unrecognized. That is because stress is a silent killer. It does not "shout" or send many warning signs that your health is being put at risk. Rather it acts swiftly and profoundly, often through heart attacks, strokes, brain aneurysms, and cancer.

The Japanese have recognized that many deaths are the direct result of stress. The phenomenon of sudden death from severe working conditions and stress is so prevalent in their society that they have coined a term for it: *karoshi*. It translates literally to "overwork death."

We are educated to believe that a certain amount of stress benefits our work performance. This idea is entirely deceiving. There is no form of stress that benefits you. This idea stems from the traditional thinking that we perform better when we activate our "fight or flight" response system. In today's world, we rely on this system regularly to boost our energy and concentration. The problem with this is that it was an evolutionary response to life or death circumstances, a tool for survival. In earlier centuries, it was seldom used. We now rely on this physiological reaction on a regular basis—to finish an Excel chart or a presentation, to make a phone call, or to deliver bad news. We must recognize that relying on fight or flight has consequences and puts strain on the body.

Every day, I work to guide working people to lower their levels of stress, to manage employees who have "burned out," to help people with severe depression find light and appreciation of their lives once more. Stress gets worse day after day and moves faster than I had ever imagined. Unlike tuberculosis, polio, and other epidemics we've faced, there will never be a simple cure for stress.

The Speed of the World

With all the developments in modern technology, time seems to be running faster than ever. Why has the hurricane of stress overtaken our lives, and why are we being trained to live with this infernal speed? In our economic system, profit maximization is the goal. Employers ask their employees to work faster, harder, and more efficiently, often with little added incentive or reward.

We have lost our sense of balance, and working has become a cultural obsession. When asked how we are doing, we often reply, "I'm busy," as if "busy" is a synonym for "well." Our society has given in to the thinking that we should feel guilty if we are not working ourselves to our personal limit. We live in a mental prison. If we lose anytime for productivity—if we don't finish our to-do list or forget to run an errand—we don't feel well. And if we are not engulfed in the obsession with time, we worry that we are not normal, that we are sick. All our energy is spent thinking that we are saving time and energy for the future. We want to work faster, eat faster, move faster, think faster, and know faster.

But take a moment to examine your life: Have you ever

stopped running? Perhaps when you went on a vacation you felt less worried, but this is a temporary effect. The time we think we are saving we often just fill with other "time-saving" activities. The brain and body are never given time to rest—and sleep and rest are two very different things.

Albert Einstein proved that time does not exist. Time depends on our perception of time. If we are present in our lives, we create a dilatation of time. Mysteriously, we feel we have more time. It is not a sensation, but a reality. Time depends on what we do with our time. It is a micro and macro reality on the planet, created and perceived by each individual.

It is only when we face the threat of death, a burnout, or a severe sickness that we realize how life is so short and so precious. It is only then that we choose to see that the wheel of time can be slowed down. We see that we feel better when we take time to appreciate the little things. And it is a very noticeable and measurable change. I have helped many people in hospitals during their final days. Many of the final words spoken by these clients are along the same lines: "It was so fast, I did not see my life moving before me." Bewildered by their regrets, they pass the same way they lived—without consciousness. This blind way of living is considered deep suffering in the teachings of the process of reincarnation.

We can see our future by looking at our present.

Instead of being "busy," we can say we have busy schedules, but we are feeling very well! Every day I teach how it is possible to work with less effort and less stress. I was fascinated to see how my rinpoche (teacher in Buddhist tradition) had a lot of work, an incredibly demanding schedule, but he was never stressed. You could see how he was free from the obsession of time. He was happy to teach and to help many people, but he never considered stress necessary. This is now one of the foundations of my teachings.

The Opposite of Our Goal

What is our goal? To be happier at work, and to be more productive with less effort. What do we need for this to happen? To have a clear mind, in order to memorize and synthesize information more easily; to connect to our intuition; and to make better decisions. For this to happen we need to reduce our stress levels, which in return will clear our minds, give us confidence, and make us feel well once again.

Our goals are clear, yet we work in a manner that is counterproductive to reaching our goal.

Every minute that we feel stressed we send negative neurochemical messages to every cell of our body, inhibiting the cells from functioning at their true potential. We destroy our neurons, our intellectual capacities, and our health. As my friends Dr. Natalie Trent at Harvard University and Dr. Mario Beauregard at the University of Arizona explain, we underestimate how much poison one minute of stress sends to our organs, muscles, and cells.

When the neurochemical message is sent to the cells, they work harder and faster, creating long-lasting fatigue. We feel a chronic dissatisfaction as we push our mental and psychical capacities, hoping for an outcome that seldom arrives. This cycle leaves us sad, and when repeated it leads us to depression and even suicidal tendencies.

Pushed by the speed of the world, we usually don't pay

attention to stress. We know we dislike the way it feels, but we continue to live with it because it is all we know. We continue to allow guilt about unfinished tasks and the distorted view of time to guide our decision to continue in this cycle.

Perhaps the most troubling misunderstanding about stress is that we fail to recognize it as a killer. Stress is the source of the major causes of death, including heart attacks, cancer, brain aneurysms, and many other types of trauma. Often we say a person died from an illness, but we don't see that the cause of that illness is rooted in the mind and our decision to feel anxious and stressed.

We are taught to accept a totally false perception of our reality. We think that to be stressed is normal.

It's not.

We are at a critical time. What is the cost of doing business? Surely not human lives.

The Cliché Version of Meditation

I jokingly open my remarks at many conferences by saying, "I don't like meditation." The word *meditation* conjures a clichéd image developed by Western society. We immediately picture a quiet mindfulness practice with the body in lotus position, hands open, palms facing upward, and eyes closed. Deep breathing and even chanting are usually included in this myth as well. When I spent three years in a monastery, I never saw any monks practicing *that* type of meditation. Monks find it amusing when tourists visit the monastery expecting to see everyone practicing yoga and chanting! This is a Western fantasy perpetuated through media and film.

This cliché version of meditation is probably what you've tried—and I don't say it will not benefit you. I, too, have tried this method. But as you may have experienced, it is not at all adapted to emergency situations and cannot easily be practiced in daily life, especially at the workplace.

A friend of mine, a dedicated meditation teacher, once said to me, "People are so stressed because they don't take time to meditate." This is the most common justification for why students' meditation practice declines or stops altogether. I contemplated this issue for many years, looking for a solution for my students and for the much larger world of professionals plagued by stress.

Is it realistic to tell the millions of people who are overworked, exhausted, and broken by stress, "You must change your life. Find thirty minutes or an hour to sit quietly with no interruptions or commitments, clear all the thoughts in your mind, and be at peace"? This, too, seems like a fantasy. If you take care of your family, work long hours, go to school, and so forth, you are probably already pushing your body and your schedule to their limits.

And yet it has been proven that meditation is transformative for the mind, body, and spirit. From lowering anxiety and increasing memory to reducing blood pressure and boosting your immune system, we know meditation works! But day after day passes and we have yet to practice, and even more importantly, we have not made practicing routine in our lifestyles.

Why wouldn't we do something that benefits us? We drink water. We go to the gym. We eat healthy food and monitor our weight. We try to get ample rest. We keep the body clean and take medicine to prevent illness. We educate ourselves. We try to be kind.

So why haven't we added meditation to this list?

I usually start with a simple metaphor. If you know to shower every day to clean your body, why don't you do anything to clean your mind? After all, the mind is the motherboard for all that we do and all that we are.

The meditation practices we have learned, the cliché we all imagine, are simply not adapted for the life we live today. Many spiritual teachers, including monks and nuns, have the privilege of stable accommodations and don't have to worry about living expenses. They are fortunate enough to enjoy a protected life, away from the harsh realities many of us face. They don't live with a high level of daily stress, and as a result their teachings on stress are about a reality they do not live. Furthermore, they underestimate how times have changed and how teachings must be adjusted for modern life before they eventually become obsolete.

If you've found a stress-relief technique that works for you, great! If you are not sure your technique is working, there is a simple test to determine if you should continue. In your daily life, at home, at your workplace, are you less stressed when you practice your techniques? Can you say your thoughts are running less feverishly? Do you find that your emotions "yo-yo," happy one moment and devastated the next? Can you control your emotions, or do they control you? Is your mind clear? Are you happy? Deeply happy? If you've answered "yes," your practice works perfectly. But if you don't feel less stress at work and at home, your practice does not work.

The goal of mindfulness practice is not to become more religious, but to be happier and more present to your life. The goal of life is to be alive. Just alive. Deeply alive. Peace is our ultimate nature. We seek it desperately because we know it is how we are naturally designed to live. We seek the quiet of nature because we are made of the elements. Our aspiration for peace is deep and sincere; the cliché version of meditation is just the opposite.

The Roots of Stress

Of course, the roots of stress are money problems, family difficulties, career advancement, and so forth. However, it is our false perception of stress, our need to attach ourselves to stress, literally *our addiction to stress,* that creates our suffering.

When I teach in schools, I always ask children, "What does the word *meditation* mean?" While their initial answer is "sleep," usually the one that follows is the cliché of mediation, as I have just described it. They sit on the floor, hands open in the air, and giggles fill the room. Even children recognize that this form of meditation is a fantasy. Even as children we are taught that peace is merely a fantasy: You can find it on vacation, but not in your daily life.

One day a Buddhist monk who is a friend of mine came to New York for the first time. As a monk, he was interested in finding a place to try to spend time alone quietly. I offered to show him some of the local studios, and when we arrived, he said, "What Buddhism is this? American people have made a new form of Buddhism I have never even seen in a monastery! When did this Buddhism happen?" He laughed as he watched the class being taught, and he laughed even harder when we saw each student leave more frustrated and anxious than they had entered. When I told him how much each class cost, he nearly fell to the floor in hysterics. It was a startling moment of two worlds colliding, and I will never forget it.

We never see a person peacefully sitting in Times Square. We only see "peace" depicted as a two-week yoga retreat in a secluded mountain range advertised on a magazine cover in the check-out line at the grocery store.

We have forgotten that peace is everywhere.

And better yet, it's free!

Peace is our nature, and we know this deeply in our hearts. Have you ever had a great day? On those days, you radiate joy. All those around you feel this joy; it is simply contagious. This joy brings you peace. You feel well in mind, body, and spirit. Without realizing it, you are balancing your hormones, boosting your immune system, and keeping your body healthy. Apples are delicious, but a smile a day can also help keep the doctor away! You know this feeling. You've experienced this peace, and you seek out this peace because it is your true nature. It is how you were created. You were made to be happy. Unfortunately, we have grown far from our true nature, and I am hoping that in times of distress, this book can help bring you back.

We must relearn the difference between true inner peace and the "peace" we fantasize about. Inner peace, true peace, can be found anytime, anywhere.

The goal of *Meditation for Daily Stress* is to correct a false perception of our reality. Peace is like oxygen; it is everywhere and accessible to anyone at anytime.

If you follow the practices I have created you will discover that you can use breathing and visualizations to ground yourself anytime you feel unwell. The key to the practices in this book is that they seek to cure the roots of stress, not just the symptoms.

The more we practice meditation (or any mindfulness technique that takes us outside of our daily situation), the more deeply our brain is imprinted with the idea that peace is always with us. The more we give in to stress, the more our health declines. If we do not stop the cycle, surely we will burn out, broken by overworking our minds and bodies. We will become dependent on substances we don't need, and in time, we will find ourselves in an emergency situation.

Meditation is not a posture or breathing pattern; it is a change in the perception of daily life.

To help you see past the cliché version of meditation, I have bridged my teachings with the outstanding findings and studies of neuroscience. My dear friends, Dr. Mario Beauregard, PhD, and Dr. Natalie Trent, PhD, have assisted me in deeply understanding how we can change our thinking, brain chemistry, and more through meditation. Specifically, we have collaborated to find the best way to meditate for those suffering from high stress levels at work. In addition, we've also been able to focus on helping high-risk communities, including children, and those facing illness.

Meditation has typically been seen as a luxury, an indulgence. But there is no expense involved in meditating, and there is no expense to finding peace. Wealth can buy you a nice vacation, but any peace you find on holiday will be fleeting unless your perception of peace is deeply changed.

Whether I am teaching Google employees, military veterans, parolees at the Amity Foundation, or students at Harvard, there is one commonality among all my students: They are all looking to feel peace. They are overwhelmed by daily tasks and running thoughts. They cannot find a way to be mindful in their daily lives. They have tried the teachings of meditation, yoga, mindfulness-based stress reduction (MBSR), and other stress-relief techniques, but they have not been able to incorporate these tools into their schedule long-term.

Many of my students say the greatest challenge in practicing these techniques is finding the time. I think the problem is bigger than that. Most of the mindfulness exercises or classes offered are not adapted to everyday issues. It's great to chant "om" with your neighbor, but when you leave that comfortable setting and that "om" becomes "om, my god," you quickly lose your sense of peace and spiral back into stress.

Maybe this is the circumstance in which you find yourself, and the reason you've chosen to read this book. Desperate for a solution, many overworked professionals decide to go on a retreat or practice yoga, but the moment they return from this blissful place, they are stressed again. When they go back to their lives, the blues take over, and they often feel worse than they did before. Clearly, a temporary fix will not break the cycle of stress.

Stress is something we become accustomed to, and it can become an addiction. The same way the mind craves cigarettes or a glass of wine, the mind yearns for situations that generate stress and repeats this pattern until the cycle becomes intolerable.

The key to controlling stress, staying relaxed, and finding peace is using a wellness practice that is incorporated into your daily life to relieve stress as it is happening rather than before or after. This is my intention for the practices in this book.

Presentation of the Practices

Each practice has three elements

Part 1: Diagnostic

We must look honestly at our situation. Stress is a mental disease. When we are stressed, we have a severe, dangerous sickness. We reduce our will to live. We must face our situation through the same process as when a doctor says to us that we are very sick. There are three steps to diagnosis:

We refuse (denial). We can't admit our sickness. We refuse to see the situation. We hide. We don't care. Or, even worse, we think it is normal. Why? Because all around us people are stressed. The more we are surrounded by those who are stressed the more stressed we become, the sicker we become, and the more we refuse to admit the truth.

We are upset (anger). The second step is to be upset at the world. Why me? Why am I so sick? How is it possible? I try to take care of myself. Sometimes I play sports or practice yoga. I try to eat organic foods. I have parties with my friends. I love the arts. I try to be spiritual. It doesn't matter. My doctor says that because of stress, I have a deep sickness. I am sending poison to all of my cells regardless of my lifestyle.

We accept (abandonment). Of course, the more we are in denial, the more upset we become. And the more I teach, the more I see how we underestimate our situation with stress. It is only when we crash that we realize the seriousness of the situation.

When we have that crash, we feel abandoned. We listen to our body, and it says, "I am out. I do not have enough energy this morning." We can't concentrate. We are broken, depressed. We say, "I am fed up! Help me, please, what can I do right now to feel less stress, to feel better?"

This step is the most important moment. We must embrace this moment. If we embrace it, we start our healing process. It is our highest teaching, our blessing. When we are broken, we enter our abandonment. We enter into the journey of healing. How can we heal? We open our ego to be helped. We have crossed through the denial and the anger.

To accept our condition and to choose to do something about it is half of the healing process. When we are broken by stress, we want to stand up. What can we do? It's counterintuitive, but we should sit down and look deeply into ourselves. When I teach at the Amity

Foundation in Los Angeles, I'm fascinated by the humility of my students, my friends, who are parolees, drug and alcohol abusers, and the homeless. They sit down, and I mean they really sit down.

When we are in an emergency stress situation, if we are able to practice any mindfulness exercises, like the ones in this book, we feel better immediately. Our broken moment becomes our rebirth. In theology, we say it is our resurrection.

Part 2: Visualization

We are what we think, what we visualize, what we suggest, and what we say. Every visualization in this book comes from a very strict lineage from the Hesychia and Nyingma Buddhism traditions, which are pure sources of spirituality.

At work, in our daily lives, on our computers and cell phones, we can use images to stimulate our minds and invite healing.

Part 3: Guidance

We will use guidance. It can be in the form of spoken or written words. Why do we need it? Because during practice it is very difficult to focus our minds. For each practice, you will read the guidance first. After that you can close your eyes and abandon your mind to the mental picture of the guidance. When you read the guidance, it is important to read slowly. Read the words deeply. Feel the breath between two words. Feel the memory, the transmittal of consciousness, through the words.

Words are more than simple letters and syllables. They are energies. So the more time we take to read deeply, the more we activate the energy sent in them. Like a painting, where we feel the emotion that a painter has given from his or her heart, we can feel energy in a word. When I am writing this book, the guidance I write is from the bottom of my heart, from my prayers, which are in every single word. Every day I bless my computer. I take care to read in a quiet environment. My mind is calm, and I am sure that when you read this book, you can feel it. What can we do when we want to feel energy more deeply? We can close our eyes. We are inside ourselves. If you close your eyes now, for just a few seconds, you will feel the meaning of this paragraph more deeply. You will be more connected to the energy through the words. Close your eyes, now. Just for a few seconds.

Open your eyes. You see how easy it is to be connected?

We will use guidance in this way. You will read, as slowly as you can, and right after you finish, close your eyes a few seconds, just to feel more deeply what you have read, to feel the energy in every word, to feel the energy beyond the words, to feel the inspiration, the lineage. I explain the importance of lineage and the Tibetan concept of *phowa*, or transmission of energy, on page 179.

You can even record the guidance very softly with your voice and listen with your earphones. Or you can go on my website, michelpascal.tv, to hear the guidance through videos or audio.

practice *1*   *meditate like the horizon*

Unplug your brain when it is
running all time

Diagnostic

One of the most devastating symptoms of stress is our inability to stop constantly thinking. Thoughts run through our brains day and night. We are slaves of an infernal machine. Every day, we overextend our cognitive capacity, leaving our minds and bodies overstimulated. The pressure to achieve our goals—whether it is to make more money, to stay connected though our phones and computers, to excel in meetings—gets greater and greater, year after year.

For the past hundred years or so, human exhaustion was mostly physical, due to the demands of manual labor; now our fatigue is mostly psychological and neuronal. Neuroscientists like Dr. Mario Beauregard believe that there is a link between our brains running all the time and degenerate illnesses, like Alzheimer's disease and Parkinson's disease. In a few years, we may see young people struggling with these illnesses usually associated with old age. Just as we can maltreat a muscle with overwork or an organ with alcohol or drugs, we affect the brain's ability to function if we don't take proper care of it. This is especially true in today's world, where we are constantly facing mental stimulation—we probably spend more time looking at a screen than we do into one another's eyes.

This fatigue, this discomfort, day after day, year after year, becomes a neurochemical addiction: We are fooled into thinking that higher stress levels result in a higher quality of work. However, through neuroscience we now know it is exactly the opposite. When we are stressed, we tire more quickly, our minds become cloudy, and we have reduced access to intuition and a lower ability to synthesize information. Making decisions becomes fearful, difficult, and anxiety-prone. When our brain is running all the time, we are in a state of mental confusion, because we have too many toxins. And we find ourselves unable to separate our situations at work from our private lives.

During a typical workday, we receive an overload of information over eight or nine hours of intense and high activity. When we come back home we need to rest, but instead we keep our brains active. We are unable to stop our overworked brains.

We act in the exact opposite manner of that which would benefit our mind, body, and spirit. Just as we take time to exercise and stretch our bodies, we must take time to release the tensions in the mind. This expansion of neuroplasticity in the brain is essential to our mental health.

We would all like to stop this machine and breathe. We would all like to put a stop to this pattern and we are drawn to meditation, yoga, and other techniques to do so. We have tried these experiences, but when we go back to our workplace, our daily life, the benefits simply disappear.

We are in an emergency situation, and we don't know any

practices or teaching that will help us cope. We allow stress to slowly destroy us. We need something that we can do to feel better immediately.

We have no choice but to face our computer and be surrounded by pressure and colleagues engulfed in their own stresses. And on top of this, we are simply exhausted; mentally and physically we feel we are unable to do anything, really. And this feeling of hopelessness is at best devastating, and at worst, lethal. It's time to give your mind a rest and to break the pattern of stress addiction.

Visualization: Meditate Like the Horizon

When our brain is running all the time, what is our fantasy? To unplug. To feel fewer waves of emotion, less "up and down."

We need our brainwaves to register as "flat," to reduce our running thoughts to a flat line.

Pure. Quiet. Uncomplicated.

We can meditate like the horizon.

To visualize a horizon, follow the two steps below.

1. Stabilize your mind. Imagine you are seeing a scan of your thought patterns. See the machine that is used to measure the movement of these thoughts. Perhaps it's similar to the way we see a heartbeat; visualize a machine with a black screen and a green line that moves in sync with your thoughts. Now, see this same green line as horizontal, flat. In this moment, our thoughts have stopped, we focus on this visualization, and we unplug from the chaos around us immediately.

The picture of the horizon is a straight line, with no waves, no jolts, no complications.

It is a relaxing mental picture because of its purity and stability. We know that the geometry of this line structures our mind, and hence, changes our cognitive process. And the change is registered in every one of our cells.

In the Middle Ages, workers built cathedrals with special attention and regard to geometry, particularly sacred geometry. They did not design buildings of worship with only beauty in mind; lines were chosen to mimic the sensation of the horizon. This is also true in the Japanese Zen tradition. The lines of the tatami are used to create a sensation of simplicity and purity, like the horizon, to counteract the jolts of information that agitate the mind. So to visualize the horizontal line, the flat brainwave, allows us to find peace immediately.

2. See beyond our reality. Most of the time, we are inside of our daily stress, like being in the ocean, in the waves, and we can't see the horizon. In this situation our vision, our perception of life, is just waves. Visualizing a horizon helps us experience an expanding reality. Yes, we have our problems and our stress, but we see that there is life beyond this stress. The more we visualize the horizon, the more readily we open our minds to another dimension, to a greater perspective. It is like a dilatation of our consciousness.

Guidance

I have written the instructions below to mirror the way I guide meditation in person. You will feel all my heart, all the inspiration from my lineage, from the monastery where I studied, and from my masters, like Chepa Dorje Rinpoche. The energy will be transmitted through the guidance, and this is so for each practice in this book. This is the idea of *phowa*, a Tibetan term for the transmission of energy from teacher to disciple.

Just before reading the guidance, take a deep breath, center yourself, and respect this practice, this time you have taken to take care of yourself. Next, read the guidance. It takes just a few seconds. Then close your eyes for a few seconds and remember what you have read; let it come easily, with little effort. The mind is intelligent: It will choose to remember the right information in a way that resonates with you. The guidance is like a prayer, a mantra, to structure your practice, to be connected with the positive, creative energy and the universe around us.

Exercise 1: Unplug

Begin just as you are, sitting down at your desk,
facing your computer,
or in whatever circumstance you find yourself.
Simply stop what you are doing.
Snap your fingers three times, like the sound of three gongs
     in a monastery.
This is the start of your practice.
At this time, close your eyes.
Visualize your brain activity as a flat, horizontal line.
Totally flat.
When you read these words, "Visualize your brain activity as
     a flat, horizontal line,"
you stimulate the picture in your brain,

and you send a message to every cell in your body,
and their energy will become "flat," following suit.
You feel more relaxed and quiet.
Every cell in the body is connected to every emotion.
Movement in your emotions is registered in every cell.
So when you visualize your brain activity as flat,
every cell will feel it.
It will be more effective than looking at a beautiful picture,
a real sensation throughout your body.
See the "screen" of your brainwaves.
Flat.
No thoughts.
No jolts.
No tension.
No perception.
Nothing.
A flat brainwave.
A pure line.

If thoughts appear,
you will do . . .
nothing.
Nothing at all.
No attachment to your thoughts.
Just let them come and go,
allow them to move naturally,
as clouds in the sky.
You can choose to see these thoughts as "jolts,"
jolts on the dark screen.

Just mechanical.

Up and down.

Agitation.

Return once again to the flat line.

This will allow you to unplug once more.

Be diligent,

return to the flat line as soon as you can.

You are ready to begin the practice. Start with three snaps, then close your eyes. Take a moment to remember what you have read. Do not worry if you cannot remember each detail. This fixation on details is simply another way for the mind to continue to cycle through its preoccupation with running thoughts. Just close your eyes, take a few seconds to remember what has resonated with you, and begin your visualization.

There is no specific amount of time that you should practice this visualization. Stay with your eyes closed as long as you are comfortable. You will feel naturally when it is time to stop. It is normal to lose your visualization after a few minutes, mostly because our mind is not used to the silence, and we become, well, fed up, for lack of a better expression.

The more you practice, the easier you will feel when your body and your mind need to stop. Sometimes you will practice for just a few seconds, or minutes, or more. It is à la carte. The best discipline is to practice every day, regardless of whether you are at work or at home, on a bus or in a park. Any effort at mindfulness, at slowing down, is important for your freedom and happiness.

Now you can close your eyes and visualize your flat brain activity.

CLOSE YOUR EYES

~

PRACTICE

~

OPEN YOUR EYES

How do you feel?

Immediately more relaxed. With the brainwave visualization, you have stretched the neuroplasticity of your brain. It's like a muscle after a strenuous effort, so you feel more relaxed.

How are your senses?

Around you, the light may seem brighter. The colors may seem more real. You can touch something with your fingers. The tactile sensation on your fingers is more sensitive, more vivid. Why? Because when you practice with visualization, your inner world becomes quiet, and immediately your senses are heightened. When you visualize how to stop your brain from running all the time, you are more present to your life. You feel better. It's just that simple.

Would you like to know if your visualization worked? It's simple to determine. If, just after the practice, you see more clearly, you listen more clearly, and your tactile sensation is more vivid, that means your visualization has begun to work very well.

If this has not happened, do not fret. As with all things, practice makes perfect. The cycle of running thoughts is a difficult one to break. Be gentle on yourself and continue to practice.

I urge you not to become discouraged. You are the master of your mind, not its slave.

Continue practicing and your mind will strengthen its capacity to be quiet. As with physical exercise, over time you will become stronger and find these practices easier.

Exercise 2: For Running Thoughts

Exercise 2 is an extension of Exercise 1. The first practice was good, but perhaps you would like to feel a deeper sensation of peace and more control of your mental activity, until you can meditate like the horizon (Exercise 3). After the first practice you may see that your running thoughts rush back into your mind. This is normal. Remember, stress and running thoughts are neurochemical addictions. Just as someone who has recently quit smoking may crave a cigarette, your mind needs to feed off of stressful thoughts. To catch these running thoughts after your first practice, follow the visualization below.

Again, begin by reading the guidance, repeat the three snaps, and then close your eyes and visualize.

> Begin by visualizing an active brainwave.
> Yes, your running thoughts on the dark screen,
> as we described them in Exercise 1. See them on the screen,
> but don't judge them.
> Do not be angry with yourself.
> As you visualize your brain activity,
> every thought has its own jolt.
> There is an evolution of each thought
> visualized as a normal curve

with a beginning (the line ascends) and an ending (the line
    returns to flat).

It is a mechanism.

Visualize this jolt.

You will see it clearly.

It is an undulation in your brainwave.

Suddenly you visualize your brainwave as flat.

You unplug.

And immediately the jolt will stop.

Flat.

No perception.

No sensation.

If another thought comes into your mind, like a new jolt,

mentally focus on it.

Follow its pattern

and, when ready, return to visualizing the flat brainwave

so you unplug this jolt,

this disruptive thought.

CLOSE YOUR EYES

~

PRACTICE

~

OPEN YOUR EYES

How do you feel? When you open your eyes, see how the colors,
the light, the sounds around you are more vivid. Why? Because you
have stretched your brain, so your senses are more developed.

You can be proud of yourself. With visualization you have stopped the mechanism of undulation, the high and low. You may think it is only modest progress, but maybe for the first time in your life you have started to recognize and control the process of stressful thinking. You have begun to reverse this dangerous habit. You have consciously taken control of your thoughts.

Yes, it is a modest amount of progress, and it may feel new for you. But this little bit of progress proves that you have started to modify your cognitive activity. It proves an incredibly important point: It is possible to change your thoughts with the power of your own mind. This is not a hollow claim to spiritual enlightenment, but a reality that you can experience. And don't forget that every cell in your body has felt this modification. Every cell has received the signal, the neurochemical message that you are not a slave of your brain, but rather its master. This knowledge can save your life.

Why are we so stressed? Because we think it is impossible to be less stressed. We have accepted stress and its effects as "normal." With this visualization you see how it is easy to make vital changes to your thinking. I hope this gives you hope, like a light at the end of a tunnel. This hope can bring you happiness. It should give you a sensation of freedom. Anytime you like, you can repeat this practice and develop the comfort of quieting your own thoughts.

One more time, OK?

Feel free to organize your practice according to your schedule. Yes, you must practice every day; discipline is the key. But this discipline must be motivated by your desire to be happy, creative, and relaxed.

Exercise 3: Meditate Like the Horizon

This third exercise asks you to see the brainwave line clearly, like a horizon line, and then to transform this line into the horizon.

So, first, read this guidance, and then take a deep breath, as a sign of respect for yourself and this teaching.

Begin just as you are, sitting down at your desk,
facing your computer,
or in whatever circumstance you find yourself.
In a few seconds, you will close your eyes,
to visualize your flat brainwave.
Immediately you will see this flat line,
a pure line,
no jolts, no thoughts.
A line like the horizon.
Like the horizon on a calm ocean.
Pure. Infinite.
Freedom.
No sensation.
No perception.
Just the horizon.
Pure freedom.

CLOSE YOUR EYES

~

PRACTICE

~

OPEN YOUR EYES

How do you feel? As with the previous exercises, you should feel more relaxed and more present to the things around you and the sensations and space inside of you. You realize that at your workplace, in your office, you can feel this peace; you can stretch your brain and experience an expanding reality. It is a revolution. Yes, you can feel space, peace, and stability like the horizon, without effort, just by the power of visualization.

Exercise 4: Practice with Your Eyes Open, in Any Situation

Do you ever find yourself at work, in a meeting, unable to concentrate on what is happening in the moment? Too many thoughts are crossing through your mind. You would like to practice the horizon visualization, but you can't close your eyes, because there are people around you. This meditation exercise is specifically created for those situations. Spirituality must be very concrete, adaptable, and usable in all circumstances. In my Buddhist lineage, the Nyingma tradition, we have a lot of practices that are done with our eyes open. We developed the capacity to be in a relaxed state, like sleep, but with our eyes open.

In fact, many high lamas have glasses, not because their vision is impaired, but because they hide their eyes during certain practices. Many of these practices allow the lamas to send their pupils backwards, only revealing the whites of their eyes. Naturally, this would scare many people, so glasses are used to protect the lamas and those around them.

We know that we are what we visualize. So you can be what you see and use what you see to meditate like the horizon. You have seen that in the guidance the horizontal line enables you to unplug from your thoughts. So if you can focus on any horizontal line with your eyes open, while you are in a meeting with managers or coworkers, it is possible to have the same results. Remember, sacred geometry can be embraced anywhere, anytime.

For example, look at the edge of a desk, the border of the keyboard on your computer, the edge of a window or table—any horizontal line will work. And during your meeting, just watch this line, like a brainwave, a horizon, inside you. Find your horizon.

Before trying it in front of others, you can practice on your own with your eyes open. Just concentrate during this practice. One of the benefits of closing your eyes is that it removes distraction. However, practicing with your eyes open can be as effective, and a great test of your ability to slow your thinking. You do not need to remember a specific guidance; rather, focus for a few seconds on a line, and it will reactivate your visualization from earlier exercises.

Exercise 5: Meditate Like the Horizon with Your Smart Phone or Computer

If you have just a few seconds at your workplace, in the subway, on a train, or in a plane, you can use your cell phone, iPad, or computer to practice this visualization. Find an image of a horizon, or a flat line, that resonates with your idea of "peace," and save it to your desktop or somewhere on your device that is easy to access.

If you leave this picture as your home page, or as your desktop background, it will regularly reactivate visualization on a subconscious level. Of course, you can practice with eyes open or closed and read the guidance just as before.

Exercise 6: Meditate Deeply Like the Horizon with Your Breathing

If you can find the time, even once a day or once a week, to expand on this visualization, your ability to stop your running thoughts will strengthen.

We become what we visualize. When you read my guidance, your mind sends a new, peaceful message to your body. But if you read a violent book or watch a violent movie, you send a negative cognitive message to all of your cells.

If you meditate like the horizon, you can really become the horizon. How? With your breath. Take a deep breath in and exhale deeply, as deeply as your body will allow. You can visualize your breath like the horizon line; inhale it, breath after breath, and the horizon will be deeper and deeper inside you.

Before you close your eyes, read this guidance and take a deep breath to respect these words, written like a prayer or a mantra to guide you.

As you inhale, take in all your thoughts.
As you exhale, see all your thoughts leave you.
You are left inside with a calm horizon.
A perfect line.
An infinite stability
inside you.

And the more you exhale, deeper and deeper,

the easier these thoughts leave you,

the easier you will see this line and feel the horizon of peace
within.

Like the horizon, there are no perturbations,

no thoughts, no jolts.

You become the master of your thoughts.

And you feel more freedom.

Interior freedom.

Peace.

Like a pure line,

simplicity finds you,

just like the calm horizon.

practice **2** _meditate like a dolphin_

Discover your inner peace
in high-stress moments

Diagnostic

We feel stressed because we were educated with a false
perception of peace. We think we can find peace only in a quiet
place, like a yoga room, a monastery, or outdoors. But this is not
true. In the midst of noise and stress, we can find peace. How? If
we learn to discover and feel the difference between the world
outside and the world inside.

What does this mean?

All around us, we have the world outside. The noise, the
stress, the tension, the responsibilities, and so forth. In general, we
function to serve the world outside. Stress is ubiquitous because
we focus too much on the external world and not enough on the
internal world. We are not present to our life. So where are we?

We focus on the outside world because we have been
taught to, from the time of early childhood. We focus on good
manners, our education, our careers, and building families. All
of these things are important. However, we also focus on the
outside world because we are attracted to distractions in the
form of endless amounts of moving information via the Internet
and social media. So we observe, judge, project, and give all our

attention and concentration to the outside world. Our attraction to the outside world has become more than a mere interest; it is an addiction. We are possessed by the speed at which the world moves, and we feel we must always be looking outward to avoid "missing something."

Ironically, while we continue looking for this "something," we lose sight of the thing that is most important: the world inside.

The world inside is another world. It is a world that we rarely seek to explore, a world we cannot imagine exists because we have not been taught to value it. There is quiet space within us all, another dimension of our being. Like the ocean water beneath the waves, there is a world inside of us with great depth, beauty, purity, and silence that often goes unnoticed. This world inside is our soul, the representation of our spiritual dimension.

When we don't feel present or grounded, it is because we ignore our soul, our world inside. As we spend more time and energy fixated on the outside world, we lose touch and become absent to our deepest dimension. Our ultimate peace, our holy shrine, our ultimate nature is inside us and nowhere else. Why? Because the outside world is a world of distraction, jolts, futility, and "ups and downs."

You may wonder, is it possible to feel peace from the outside world? For instance, if you are offered your dream job or you earn a degree, is it wrong to feel peace from these things? No, of course, you will feel peace and joy from these things—but peace linked to material objects and career milestones is temporary, fleeting.

The only peace that can be found regardless of life's circumstances is the peace that is inside of us. Peace is not found by fixating on the past or the future. The peace inside us can only be found and enjoyed in the now, in the present moment. When we are inside of our soul we feel better, quieter, and centered immediately.

It's natural to think these two worlds are opposites, but we should think of them as complementary. Everything in life has an outside and an inside dimension. All is material and spiritual. In theology, we say that we are half human and half divine. Like the sky and the earth, we live and experience both worlds simultaneously. If we live only in the sky, we are unbalanced. We miss the concrete aspects of our nature. But if we focus solely on the earth, we feel a deep unbalance in the opposite direction; we miss the sky, our faith. We must be grounded with our roots and grow up to bloom in the sky. We must be both, because life is both, and duality is the nature of our earthly experience.

All exists in duality. This is not a spiritual or philosophical position, but a reality that has been proven by science. All is real and not real. For example, you read this book. The paper in your hands is real. It is solid. But at the same time, a scientist could prove to you that this book, this paper you hold, is actually moving, fluid, at the level of subatomic particles. All is solid and fluid. The symbol of Jesus on the cross also represents the junction between the human and the divine, Father and Son, to use those archetypes. For many centuries leading up to the present, The Christ served as an archetype of the synthesis of the human and the divine. With this practice, Meditate Like a Dolphin, we say we have two worlds— outside and inside—to represent this same concept.

We can't separate a wave on the ocean from the depth of the ocean, just as we can't separate day and night. When we do not make time to experiment with learning about our world inside, we stay at the level of the waves, the surface level, and we never discover our true depth.

When we see ourselves only as waves, we feel that our lives are missing something. We long for something we don't understand that would make us "happy." Have you ever heard someone say, "I will be so happy when . . ."? Have you noticed that when that "something" is accomplished, happiness doesn't fill the void as we thought it would? Looking for the outside world to create happiness only leads to one thing: spiritual fatigue.

What does it mean to enter into spiritual fatigue? Spiritual fatigue is the exhaustion of living without the knowledge of our interior world. In this state, our goals and accolades are determined solely by the outside world. We are tired because we are slaves of all our actions. We take the subway, go to our workplace, have fun with friends, go out to restaurants, celebrate holidays, buy new clothes—and so what? In the outside world we spend huge amounts of effort seeking satisfaction. We exhaust ourselves chasing something that is always running away or changing form.

How can we feel good when our ultimate reality—our consciousness—is not active?

When we focus only on the outside, we feel a frustration in our soul, a chronic dissatisfaction we are unable to understand. For example, we can be rich, with the best clothes, jewelry, homes, and technology, but while the ego insists these things will bring us happiness, the soul knows deeply that they will not satisfy the thirst for true, unconditional happiness.

In neuroscience, we talk about different levels of consciousness in our brain. We know that when we are focused on our inside world, such as in deep contemplation or meditation, we activate many cognitive processes not normally used. Our focus on the inside world changes our hormonal balance to allow us immediately to feel calmer, happier, and less tired.

The first time I discovered that we have two worlds, two levels of consciousness, outside and inside, it was a revelation. At ten years old, I discovered that I loved to spend time in churches. I felt peace, space, and freedom. I experienced this sensation in a very real way, without any teachings. Why? Because a church is a representation of our soul, our spiritual dimension. In theology, we say that a church is the physical representation of the place where the presence of God lives inside of us. In Buddhism, we say that our monastery is our refuge.

When I was studying in the Kopan Monastery in Nepal, I was so happy to have time to dive deeply into the world inside, to discover that there is a real space, an entire universe, inside me. When my friend Lobsang Sherab sang the prayer every morning and every evening, I felt a dilatation in my mind, flowing through my body, down to all of my cells. In a religious life, we are conscious of the world inside and connect to this world as often as possible every day. Hours are spent in prayer, meditation, or in other practices. We honor the world inside, while understanding and adapting to the world outside. The goal of religion is to help us connect to the world inside and remember that the world inside is our truth, our nature, and our source.

In describing my time in the monastery, I often talk about the difference between learning and living. In the monastic life, we learn more than just Buddhism; we live what we learn through concrete experience. For me, discovering the outside and inside worlds was a revelation, probably one of the highest teachings I have received in my life. Once it is learned and truly understood, it cannot be unlearned or forgotten. Seek the experience yourself by paying attention to the outside and inside worlds in your own life.

In the Bible Jesus says, "Go to your room, and close your door." In Christianity, when we pray we feed our inner world; we enter into our room and into a relation with The Christ, seeking his guidance and peace to help us improve our relationship with the world inside and to give us strength to face the world outside.

The saying regarding money and death is "you can't take it with you," suggesting that after death your material possessions will remain on this earth. This is a simple example of the significance of the world inside versus the world outside. We have learned to focus our energy on creating the external world of our dreams— generally speaking, financial wealth, loving relationships, beauty, and good health. Many contemporary movements in spirituality suggest that the world outside is merely an illusion, and that the only truth, the only real existence, is in the world inside.

In a monastery, when we are in contemplation or prayer, we feel this level of consciousness. When we are in contemplation we discover the world inside; we have the sensation of an ocean inside us. After we have finished our prayer, we return to the world outside. It is like when you are swimming in the ocean, submerged in the water, deep in the silence, and afterward you return to the water's surface.

When we are in nature, in the woods, on a beach, or on a mountain, this sensation of the two worlds is crystal clear. Being is nature is often regarded as a good form of therapy for PTSD and anxiety because we are removed from the distractions of the outside world and are able to focus deeply on the world inside ourselves. Typically, when we come back to our jobs after spending time in nature, our sense of wellness is fleeting. It is a difficult experience, a mix of emotions that can be confusing. For some, it manifests as depression; for others, it registers as hostility. Regardless, the experience of returning to the outside world is difficult because we feel we are leaving our true selves and our true nature behind. To travel smoothly from the inside world back to the outside requires spiritual maturity. My techniques are designed to help you locate the peace deep inside of you and then return to the outside world carrying forward the peace you have just found.

Of course, most of us don't spend the majority of our time in a monastery or in nature, but at our workplace, at home, or commuting. At the New York corporate office of Google, I taught employees how we can enjoy our lunch in silence, focusing on the world inside, despite the distractions or obligations that may exist in the outside world. For one of my students, a manager at the company, it was an incredible experience to discover that she could eat quietly, think deeply, and discover her inner world at the noisy restaurants at Google headquarters. Furthermore, she could use the distractions in the room as a measure of her ability to remain focused on the peace within, regardless of the circumstances in which she found herself.

So how can we adapt this teaching to the lives we live everyday? How can we feed our soul? How can we travel from the world outside to the world inside?

Visualization: Meditate Like a Dolphin

One morning, while swimming at Santa Monica beach in California, I saw a wild dolphin just a few meters away from me. When we have a close encounter with a dolphin we feel an incredible presence that is full of peace, love, pure compassion, and divine happiness. It is a majestic experience. I was fascinated by his presence. He was, from that moment, my spiritual teacher. Suddenly he jumped above the waves and dived into the ocean. While in the air he took a breath and then plunged, deeply. It was a lesson; the lesson I was seeking for this chapter. It shows how we can travel from the outside to the inside, and from the inside to the outside, with no problem and little effort, because it is the nature of our lives. This journey is natural to us, like going from inhaling to exhaling, from inside to outside.

The world outside is like the waves on the ocean. If we dive inside, we can discover the world beneath the surface. This is not just a theological or philosophical exercise, but a real experience, beyond religion or atheism, that we can all experience. The dolphin is also a very powerful symbol to focus our mind. We need symbols to help our minds focus on our practices. Neuroscience has proven how symbols structure information in the mind and, therefore, in our cells.

The dolphin is a universal symbol of grace—pure happiness. It is also a childhood dream, a primordial fantasy, to see a dolphin in the wild and to swim with dolphins. To have the experience is to be connected to our natural freedom.

When I teach children, they love this exercise. But this practice is also great for adults, as the first image we see of a dolphin lies in our subconscious, and we immediately reconnect to childhood. When we see a dolphin our mind is imprinted with a representation of pure grace, freedom, peace, and harmony that stays with us for the rest of our lives.

Guidance

Before you read the guidance, take a deep breath to respect this practice. Next, read the guidance. It takes just a few seconds. Then close your eyes for a few seconds and remember what you have read. Let it come easily, with no effort. A guidance is like a prayer, a mantra, to focus your mind and connect you with the positive, creative energy of the universe.

Exercise 1: Dive In

You are seated
at your desk,
or in the subway.
Wherever you are,
you don't move.
You do nothing.
You are simply present.
Your eyes are open.
If you have thoughts
calling for your attention,
you do nothing.
Thoughts are like waves on the ocean.
Always beginning,
always ending.

Around you there are many waves,
many noises,
many sources of stress
and distractions.
You can see clearly
that this is the world outside.
For the first time in your life,
you choose, now,
to visit the world inside.
It is a conscious choice.

You take a deep breath
and you close your eyes.
You hold the breath for three seconds,
just as at the swimming pool,
when you want to dive,
you breathe in and hold your breath
before jumping into the water.

Now, close your eyes a few seconds,
take this breath in,
and dive deeply inside yourself.

Continue to breathe in,
hold the breath for three seconds,
and exhale.
Visualize yourself under the water,
in the silence beneath the sea.

CLOSE YOUR EYES

~

PRACTICE

~

OPEN YOUR EYES

What do you feel? For the first time, you dived inside yourself. Can you see the difference between the world inside and the world outside? Can you separate the noise, thoughts, and distractions from your interior silence? It is a subtle sensation, but it is real. It is an incredible new perception in your life. A revelation. It is like the first time you went to the pool with your school, or to the ocean with your family, and suddenly you dived into the water, into the depth.

You open your eyes after a few minutes of practicing. As with the first practice, you decide how long to continue. If I dictate that you must practice for a specific amount of time, it puts unnecessary pressure on you. And most of the time, our schedules wouldn't allow the suggested time interval. So at the beginning, and especially at your workplace, it is easier to listen to your body and its perception of time to know when to end the exercise. When you feel that you are losing concentration, open your eyes.

The moment we breathe in and visualize that we are diving deep inside ourselves, we expand the sensation of peace in our minds and bodies. This sensation is just a first step, but this first experience can change our lives. For the first time, we have activated a new signal in our brains, in our cognitive process.

Exercise 2: Dive Deeper

The more we practice, the more we "print" a new sense of peace in our brains. This new sensation, when repeated regularly, creates a neurochemical addiction in the mind. We go from enjoying the momentary sensation of peace to searching for the sensation every day.

To begin this process of "printing" peace in the mind, read the following guidance and repeat the practice before moving on.

Start with your eyes open.
Take a deep breath.
Now, close your eyes,
and hold your breath
for just three seconds,
as you would before diving into water.
Now exhale deeply with your eyes closed.
You are in the world inside.
Feel the sensation of diving inside yourself.
Repeat the exercise again.
Now hear the silence of the ocean,
the silence of depth.
As you continue to breathe, hear the silence deep
    within you.
Breathe in deeply, hold the breath for three seconds,
and exhale, traveling deeper and deeper inside yourself.

CLOSE YOUR EYES

~

PRACTICE

~

OPEN YOUR EYES

What did you feel? You have experienced the sensation of diving deeper inside yourself. You felt more freedom, the space inside of you, a world that is infinite.

Exercise 3: Dive Like a Dolphin

With my approach to meditation, we use body and mind, breathing and mental images. Now that you have practiced diving deep with your breath, you are ready to add the visualization of the dolphin as it jumps above the waves to dive deep into the ocean. We read this guidance after a deep breath and a moment of silence to respect the teaching.

You are sitting down.
Around you there are noises, distractions.
You have learned how to dive,
so you can see the difference
between the world outside and the world inside.

Now visualize a dolphin.

He is majestic.

He is in the deep blue ocean, beneath a pure blue sky.

You meditate with him, you become a dolphin.

You inhale deeply like him.

At the surface of the ocean,

hold your breath for three seconds, just like the dolphin.

And suddenly you dive in, deep into the sea.

Into the silence.

To feel a greater sensation of silence,

dive again.

Go to the surface of the ocean.

Take a deep breath, like the dolphin.

Hold your breath for three seconds.

Maybe you hear some noises or thoughts.

That is normal.

As you dive back into the water,

return your focus to the silence within.

Leave the noises and thoughts outside of the water.

Focus within.

The silence beneath the water's surface

is the silence within you.

CLOSE YOUR EYES

~

PRACTICE

~

OPEN YOUR EYES

What do you feel? You should feel quieter and deeper immediately. Nothing is more incredible and concrete than visiting the silence within. Were you able to quiet your thoughts and distractions by leaving them above the water's surface? If you were, wonderful; if you were not able to, don't worry. Continue to practice at a pace that is comfortable to you.

Exercise 4: Smile Like a Dolphin

Why do we love dolphins? Because they smile all the time. Mother Teresa said, "Peace begins with a smile." When we smile like a dolphin, we activate more than sixty muscles in our face, and every cell in the body feels the message of happiness sent by our neurotransmitters. So now we will add the smile to the visualization of our dolphin. We read this guidance after a deep breath and a moment of silence to respect this teaching.

Begin seated at your workplace,
and smile before taking a deep breath.
Smile like a dolphin.
Smile from within.
See how your smile changes your face.
You become a dolphin,
with a beautiful, eternal smile.
Feel the love that radiates from this smile and
travels to all parts of your body,
to all the space inside of you.
It is a smile that overcomes any hurdle or circumstance.
If you are able to smile at work,

you are free.

The goal of this meditation is to be free from your daily stress.

Immediately.

Without effort.

And with your smile,

you take a deep breath,

hold this breath for three seconds,

and exhale deeply, diving into the water

and into the silence,

with your smile inside of you.

Remain quietly in the ocean

with your smile.

The peace of the ocean,

the depth of the ocean, encompasses you.

Don't move.

You are sitting down, with your smile, like a dolphin.

You feel happy, quiet, and relaxed.

You may even feel jovial, like a child.

You dive inside all of your cells with these feelings.

You feel how every cell is happy, quiet.

Return to the surface with your smile like a dolphin.

If you hear noises or have running thoughts,

acknowledge them, but leave them at the surface

of the water.

Again take a deep breath,

hold it for three seconds, and dive deeper inside
        of yourself.
If distracting thoughts continue,
picture yourself under the water.
At the surface of the water,
see your thoughts,
floating, calm, outside.
See how you live in both worlds.
Then return to your breathing,
holding the breath for three seconds before exhaling.

What a wonderful sensation to feel the world inside of you,
a world of interior freedom.

CLOSE YOUR EYES

~

PRACTICE

~

OPEN YOUR EYES

Now you know you can practice anytime, anywhere, like a dolphin.
You can travel inside of your mind to find the peace within. You
can use a smile to radiate love throughout your body. You can use
the surface of the water as a mental image, separating the world
inside from the world outside.

practice **3** *meditate like the wind
in the desert*

Create more time when you are busy

Diagnostic

Every day, we say, "I am busy." We have too many things to
do. Year after year, we are busier and busier. We have more
pressure and more responsibilities in our jobs. Why? Because
the world economy is more and more extreme. Two percent of
the population earns 98 percent of the money in our economy;
financial freedom has become nearly impossible for most people
today. Labor and fiscal competition is at an extreme that has
never been seen in society: If we want to enjoy good quality of
life, we must work paralyzing amounts to earn wages that allow
us to live comfortably. So we must work more to survive and find
ourselves too busy, unable to find time to rest, meditate, or take
care of ourselves.

We both _need_ to be busy, and we _love_ to be busy. Chasing
after time is one way our ego feels satisfied; it believes that "busy"
is a reflection of success.

When we say, "I am busy," we exist; we believe our life
has meaning. When someone asks us, "Are you busy?" we feel
uncomfortable replying no—we feel guilty. Not being busy
suggests that we don't have a future, that we lack motivation and

opportunities. Society has educated us to believe that we are nothing if we are not busy. Therefore, when we are not busy, we feel unimportant, we lack confidence, and we don't feel well.

At the same, we agree that we would like to be less busy; a busy life means less time to work, to enjoy our job, to take care of our health, to spend with our friends and family, and to love life.

If we had an extra hour added to the day—if every day could have twenty-five hours—what would we do? Immediately we would add more activities to our day. Why? Because we are trained and educated to push all the time. We are addicted to feeling busy.

So we live in a paradox. We would like to be less busy, but we are unable to stop the cycle of work, and we love to be busy. This is how we are conditioned. "Busy" also feels good because we are uncomfortable in silence; in our most primitive nature, silence, or nothing, is a characteristic of danger and death. If we don't practice spending time in silence, we grow to fear it.

I have created the following practice to help you open your perspective on "busy." The purpose of this practice is not to work against being busy, but rather to discover there is another way to work and a healthier perception of time.

There is a difference between being active and being busy. Every day, I work a lot. When people say, "Michel, you are so busy!" I reply, "My schedule is busy, not me." We cannot be busy and present to our lives, but we can be active and present to our lives. It is not a utopian idea, but a concrete reality.

How can we be very active but not feel busy or stressed? How it is possible to have another perception of time? And first of all, what is our perception of time?

Our perception of time is far too narrow; we see only a sliver of reality. Time has no start and no end. It is a continuum. Time is flux, as they say in quantum physics. We conceive a past, present, and future to define our relationship to the world around us.

For example, we can go to see a movie that is three hours long, and if it's exciting or a great story we feel time passes quickly. We can also go to see a movie that lasts ninety minutes, and time seems to drag on endlessly. The perception of time is personal and relative.

So when we say, "I am busy," when we are stressed, we compress our sense of time. At the opposite end of the spectrum, if we are present to our lives, we can discover something profound: In every instant there is eternity. Time is not temporal, or finite, but eternal. No one teaches us this understanding of time: It is eternity.

The words "I am busy" are stress inducing; our time is compressed when we speak them. You have experienced this effect, I am sure. Millions of people repeat these words every day, and as a result, millions of people compress their sense of time and the time of the planet. It's undeniable; year after year the world seems busier and busier.

But think about this: If we are able to compress time, we should also be able to expand it. We can do this once we realize that time depends on our perception of it. When I was with my spiritual teacher Jean-Yves Leloup, I was fascinated to see how he worked a lot—he traveled night and day to lecture, to participate in teachings and celebrations—and at the same time he was available, entirely free, when we had meetings together. One day I entered his cell in a monastery, and he said, "Michel, please come in, I have five minutes, five times sixty seconds, but *real* seconds, so we have all the time we need." And the meeting was wonderful. I felt that time couldn't catch Jean-Yves; he was master of his schedule and a master of his time.

Of course, when we are busy, our first priority is to organize our schedule better, to prioritize as you might with a life coach, for example. But we could also have just one meeting per day and feel very busy. So how can we stretch time? Is it possible to be very active but not busy, not so stressed?

Visualization: Meditate Like the Wind in the Desert

We can feel eternity at our workplace. For that, we need to live in eternity, with our minds (though visualization) and with our bodies (through breathing). We can re-create the environment of the wind in the desert, an everlasting and timeless sensation of nature.

The Wind

We will use the sound of our breath to mimic the wind. When we breathe deeply, we can listen to ourselves inhaling and exhaling like the wind in the desert. When we breathe like this, deeply and loudly, we reactivate the sound of the wind in the desert in our subconscious, even if we have never physically been to the desert.

The Desert

We will use the mental picture of the desert in this practice. With the sound of our breath like the wind, it will be easy to feel the sensation of the wind in the desert—at work, at our desks, or in any circumstance in which we find ourselves. We can practice like the wind in the desert in the subway, on the train, on a plane, or at home.

The practice can take a few seconds or five minutes or fifteen minutes; again, the most important thing is not the quantity, but the quality, of the practice. And if we practice observing eternity, we will feel more relaxed. We will feel the mysterious sensation that we have more time, because we are less stressed.

Guidance

Just before you read this guidance, take a deep breath to pay respect to the words below.

Exercise 1: Discover the Wind

You are sitting down,
facing your computer,
or wherever you are.
You are happy to practice,
to find your peace.
In a few seconds you will stretch your time.
You will feel eternity.

Close your eyes and breathe deeply. Loudly.
Inhale loudly, for five seconds,
and exhale loudly, for five seconds.
Listen to the sound of your breath.
It is so simple,
you just listen to the sound of your breath.
If some thoughts enter your mind,
do nothing,

just focus your concentration back on the sound
of your breath.
If you need better concentration, breathe deeper, louder.
You use this sound to bring you back inside yourself.
And second after second,
listen to your breath like the wind.
The wind of your breath is real inside of you.
Listen deeply to the wind.
Your breath is the wind.
For the first time, you discover that you can listen to
the wind of eternity inside you.
It is a miracle.
So simple, without any effort.

CLOSE YOUR EYES

~

PRACTICE

~

OPEN YOUR EYES

What do you feel? Immediately you should feel better, quieter.
When you open your eyes, you should feel your senses heightened.
The light around you is clearer, as are the colors and sounds. You
can touch your fingers together, and the tactile sensation is clearer.
The practice has worked well, and you have begun to stretch your
mind. You discover that your breath can become your spiritual
teacher, the best you could ask for, in any situation. You will
discover how simple it is to feel more relaxed, more present. Your
mind is clearer, and you will find it easier to work. You will find that

you crave this state of consciousness. Time has slowed down, and you feel recentered and present to whatever circumstance arises.

The moment you start this practice, you have already caused a change in your cognitive process, and minute after minute you will change the serotonin and dopamine in your brain. You will feel the results in every cell of your body. This is why you feel better. So read this new guidance to go deeper in your practice, to feel eternity inside you, and to realize that you can change time by changing your perception.

Exercise 2: The Wind of Eternity

Read this guidance after a deep breath and a moment of silence to respect the teaching.

> Begin just as you are, sitting down,
> facing your computer. You know that the second you
>   close your eyes
> and listen to your breath,
> deep and loud,
> you will be able to listen to the wind inside you,
>   inside your breath.
>
> Breathe deeply, loudly.
> You love this sound.
> When you breathe in full consciousness,
> you are able to listen to the wind.
> Where does this breath come from?
> Where does this air come from?

It comes from your office,
but also from the street near your office,
the city where you live and work,
the country, the continent, the planet where you are.
When you breathe deeply, when you listen to the wind,
you can see the journey of your breath, of the wind.
This wind comes from eternity, from the universe.
Suddenly you realize that your breath in your workplace
is connected to the wind of the universe.
You breathe eternity.
It is a miracle to feel your reality open up,
to feel the space that has opened in your mind.

Now you can close your eyes
and see the journey of your breath, the wind traveling
through your office, city, country, planet, and universe.
Today, now, without effort, you can feel the eternity
        of the universe
at your workplace.
It is a miracle.

CLOSE YOUR EYES

~

PRACTICE

~

OPEN YOUR EYES

What do you feel? Like you are waking from a dream? You are in
another state of consciousness. You are calmer, and the more you

practice, the deeper this sensation will be. When you connect to eternity you will feel quieter, and you will feel that your time has mysteriously dilated. You feel fresh, with more energy. You have the same amount of time, the same number of minutes, but less stress, so the minutes seem longer and you feel less pressure. You are present to this moment: a great gift.

Now we can go deeper into the practice. As always, before we begin, we take a deep breath to respect this guidance.

Exercise 3: The Desert Wind

You are sitting down,
facing your computer,
and you know that at the moment you breathe and listen to
  your breath
like the wind,
you will feel eternity.
You will enter into another state of consciousness,
another perception of time.
It will be the same time,
but lived with a new perception.

Close your eyes, breathing like the wind,
and add a visualization, a beautiful mental picture.
You see the desert.
A vast desert.
You are alone in this desert.
You are sitting down, just as you are, but you are in this
  desert.

Listen to your breath, like the wind in the desert.
You feel eternity.
An incredible eternity, without effort.
The desert surrounds you.
Regardless of where you are,
you are seated now in this desert.
You feel that all your cells feel the stillness
of being in the desert, alone, at peace.
You realize it is a miracle: With your breath like the wind,
you can sit down in the desert and listen
to the wind, to the eternity inside you.

CLOSE YOUR EYES

~

PRACTICE

~

OPEN YOUR EYES

What do you feel? Do you feel that time has been stretched? A good practice leaves you feeling calm, at ease, and connected to something greater than yourself. You look at your desk, your office, your coworkers, your family, and you realize that you can change the way you see everything around you with just a short mindfulness and breathing exercise. You have changed your perception of time.

Now let's go deeper in the final exercise. As usual, we take a deep breath before reading the guidance, to prepare our minds and respect the practice.

Exercise 4: Push Your Thoughts, Like Clouds in the Sky of Your Mind

You are sitting down,
looking at your life.
Breathe deeply, listen to the wind,
and see that you are alone
in your interior desert.
It is a wonderful sensation.
A refuge.

What do you see in this desert?
An incredible sky.
A blue sky.
This is the sky of your mind.
You discover that your thoughts are like clouds in the sky of
      your mind.
When you have many thoughts,
they can start to fill the blue sky of your mind.
What can you do to clear the mind of thoughts?
You can breathe and create a strong wind to push
the clouds out of your mind.
You realize that you think too much,
there are too many clouds in the sky.
So with this wind in the desert,
this wind of eternity,
you can push your thoughts out of the sky in your mind.

Now you see a cloud, a thought.
For example, a problem at your workplace.
Or the last problem with a loved one.
You can see this situation as a cloud in the sky of your mind.
Sitting down quietly, in your interior desert,
breathe deeply, loudly,
and visualize that with the force of your wind
you can push the clouds out of the sky of your mind.
You realize that you are in eternity,
in control of your problems, your difficulties,
and you are the master of your time.

It is an incredible sensation.
You decide to put aside any difficult thoughts
and choose to focus on eternity, peace.
You feel the relief this wind brings to your consciousness.
So you breathe again, loudly,
and listen to the wind of eternity in your sky,
and visualize pushing your stress out of your mind.
You see your stress disappear like a cloud pushed
        by the wind.

Let go of all thoughts, obstacles, and circumstances by
        pushing them like clouds in the desert sky.

You have changed your perception of time
in just a few seconds,
through deep concentration.

So now you are ready to close your eyes
and breathe like a wind in the desert,
and push your thoughts like clouds in the sky of your mind.

CLOSE YOUR EYES

~

PRACTICE

~

OPEN YOUR EYES

When we concentrate on using our own power to shift our perceptions, we change our lives in a matter of moments. We feel quiet and relaxed because we have chosen to find peace despite the difficulties we may face around us.

If you feel the need to sleep after this practice, don't be concerned. This is normal. When we undertake relaxation practices, we release tension and stress, sending the signal to our bodies that it is time to decompress. And when we practice this type of meditation, the transmission of oxygen to the brain is increased. Perhaps you even felt light-headed during your practice. Make sure you are self-aware and follow the guidance given from your body to your mind.

Now that we feel connected to eternity, our perception of time has changed, so our perception of our life has changed. Everything in our surroundings—our desk, our coworkers, our family—feels calmer. Time has not changed, but we live and experience it differently. Now we can say, "My schedule is busy—but not me."

practice **4** *meditate like the sky*

See inside yourself, develop intuition,
and make the best decisions

Diagnostic

This practice is the continuation of the wind visualization in Practice 3.

We don't take enough time each day to connect to the world inside of us. We are immersed in our thoughts, the clouds of our mind. Stress fogs our thinking, and we are unable to connect to our intuitive nature, to make the best decisions at the right time. We live in a manner that is exactly the opposite of our goal in life: to live with ease. Every day we must make decisions and live with the consequences of our choices, whether positive or negative. Clearing your mind is the first step to improving your decision making and, therefore, improving your life.

According to a Native American proverb, "Our life is like a tree: When we have problems, we prefer to focus on the leaves of the tree instead the roots of the tree." When you cure the roots there is healing; when you cure the leaves, the result is a temporary solution, and the ailment or difficulty will arise once more.

People try different types of coaching to help clear their minds. But if we are not able to see beyond our difficulties, we must admit that these techniques are not efficient enough to bring about real change, to cure the roots of the problem. This is especially true in today's world, where we need a clear mind and instant access to our intuition.

Visualization: Meditate Like the Sky

A visualization of the sky can help clear our mind, because our mind is like the sky and our thoughts are like the clouds. We have seen in Practice 3 how to push the clouds out of our mind's sky. Now we will develop this practice a little further.

In the ancient traditions, tribes carried turquoise stones because they believed it was like carrying a piece of the sky. Since ancient times, people have tried to represent the sky in art to help connect our human experience with the sky's grandeur. From mandalas to *thangkas*, from stained glass to the cross, we have always looked to the sky for comfort and connection.

Ancient tribes understood what neuroscience now proves: We are what we see, what we think, what we say, and what we visualize. Many traditional practices across all religions involve connecting to the sky to find peace. So when we choose to focus our thoughts on a blue sky, particularly when we see the sky as a representation of our mind, we mimic the clear and peaceful nature of the sky.

Wherever we are, we can take a few minutes to practice with the sky. You may find it helpful to download a picture of a beautiful blue sky on your computer screen or cell phone to use in this practice. If you see the sky it will help you to meditate like the sky. We will develop the practice for primary use in the workplace, but that doesn't mean we can't also take time to lay down in the grass and take in the pure sky above us.

On Catalina Island, in California, I organized some retreats that focus solely on rediscovering the sky. The sky is an incredible teacher, available to you night and day. We know we need to have a clear mind, like the sky, and the sky is above us, around us, and inside us all the time.

Guidance

Exercise 1: See the Sky

Take a deep breath before reading this guidance, as you might before saying a prayer.

> You are sitting down,
> and you see the sky above you
> or a picture of the sky on your computer—
> a blue sky, so pure.
>
> You are what you see.
> Immediately you feel calmer.
> You have more space.
> You feel a clarity, a stillness.
> You are inside this sky.
> You focus on the picture of the pure blue sky,
> and you feel at peace.

If you have distracting thoughts,
you know they are like clouds in your mind, in your sky.
So, you breathe like the wind in the desert,
and you push the clouds away,
like the thoughts in your mind.

You listen deeply to the sound of this wind.

If you need help concentrating, you breathe louder,
and as the sound of the wind on your lips increases, it
        becomes more real inside you.
You feel the wind as your breath.
And the more you breathe the wind of eternity,
the more clearly you see the sky, the more you become
        the sky.
Pure consciousness.

CLOSE YOUR EYES

~

PRACTICE

~

OPEN YOUR EYES

When we open our eyes, we see how the light is clearer. If we
touch our fingers together, the tactile sensation is intensified. When
we are calmer, we stretch the neuroplasticity of our brains. This is
not a poetic image but a real sensation: neuronal, psychological,
and physical.

Exercise 2: Become the Sky

Take a deep breath before reading this guidance, as you might before saying a prayer.

> You are seated in front of your computer at work,
> or at home, or during your commute, looking at your
>   cell phone.
> Look deeply into the picture of the pure blue sky.
> Around you are many noises, stresses.
> But they cannot catch you,
> because you are deep inside your sky.
> If you want to immerse more deeply in your sky, deeper into
>   this calm, you can breathe like the wind in the sky.
> You know how to breathe like the wind.
> You love this practice, it's so simple.
> You are happy that you can feel better with so little effort.
> You are present to your sky.
>
> And now you can enter deeper in relation to your sky.
> You can become the sky.
>
> When you inhale,
> you focus on taking in the pure stillness of the sky.
> When you exhale,
> you feel the presence of the sky has filled all the cells of
>   your body.

You know the sky, and you love it.
It is more than a picture, more than the sky.
This sky is your refuge, your friend, your space.
Ever present, and so kind,
the sky has the power to heal you.
You see the sky and you become more like it.

Now you feel that you have fewer thoughts in your sky.
You can breathe with your sky.
You become the sky.

CLOSE YOUR EYES

~

PRACTICE

~

OPEN YOUR EYES

It is so simple to purify our minds by moving our thoughts and connecting to the presence of the sky. The visualization of the sky is so powerful, and we want to connect in a deeper way. Why? Because we have created a new chemical addiction in our brain— an addiction that seeks this sensation of peace. When we practice in this way, we have activated regions of our brain that we usually do not use. They send positive messages throughout our cortex, which we feel throughout the body.

You are ready to go deeper into the practice of the sky.

Exercise 3: Diffuse the Sky Throughout Your Body

Take a deep breath before reading this guidance, as you might before saying a prayer.

> You are sitting down,
> contemplating your sky.
> You feel that your concentration is better.
> You know how to move the clouds as they arise.
>
> You can breathe the energy of the sky.
> You can visualize its blue color entering you
> as a ray of turquoise light, a pure light,
> bright and radiant.
> This turquoise light enters your body at your head,
> at the fontanel.
>
> You breathe, and at the same time,
> you follow this ray of pure blue light
> inside you.
> First you diffuse this blue light throughout your brain.
> Your mind is like the sky.
> Pure.
> Clear.
>
> Then you continue with your breath,
> and you follow this blue ray of light as it diffuses throughout
> the body.

It's in all your organs.

Your stomach is quiet like the sky.

Your kidneys are quiet like the sky.

Your heart is quiet like the sky.

Your pancreas is quiet like the sky.

Your liver is quiet like the sky.

You see your legs and arms, fingers and toes, quiet like
the sky.

You see the blue light, the pure sky,

this presence,

now, throughout your body.

You hold this visualization as you continue to breathe.

CLOSE YOUR EYES

~

PRACTICE

~

OPEN YOUR EYES

You feel a deeper clarity, a profound quietness. To meditate like the sky is so powerful for the mind and the body. Before, after, or between two meetings, this practice is an incredible refuge. Now, we can go deeper into the practice for the final step.

Exercise 4: See Beyond the Sky

Take a deep breath before reading this guidance, as you might before saying a prayer.

You love the sky above you, or the sky you see on your
     computer.
You feel how it diffuses into your body, into your mind.

Now you can close your eyes and see beyond the sky.
The sky is a representation.
A symbol.
A door to an expanding reality.
Everything helps you on your way,
including your visualizations.

What can you see beyond the sky?
Nothing.
A space with no concept.
No projection.
No picture.
A pure space beyond the sky.
Pure emptiness beyond the emptiness.
Pure light beyond the light.
Extinction of all concepts.
Nirvana.

God begins after the silence.

Focus on this space beyond the sky.
See how it is so still,
completely without disturbance.
This is your nature.
Peace.

CLOSE YOUR EYES

~

PRACTICE

~

OPEN YOUR EYES

To meditate deeply is an incredible experience. We see that at this stage we no longer need the support of the sky or of the blue light, because our mind is focused on something so grand, so outstanding, that we are left speechless, thoughtless.

When we meditate like this, we activate gamma rays in our brain, creating a deep sensation of relaxation. We also know that in sacred art, like religious icons, the images were meant to help us open our perspective beyond the painting, beyond the surface. This meditation has the same goal.

Using the steps above, you can get to this peace very simply. If you did not feel this peace, do not worry. We are patient and quick to forgive others, but we often forget to be patient with ourselves. Try this practice at your own pace, and do not force your mind to find peace, because you will only find frustration. Be kind with yourself, patient with yourself, and know that you can find this peace because it is your true nature—it is already inside of you.

Now, with this step, we are beyond our thoughts, connected to intelligence greater than our own. With a clear mind, you can make the best decisions using your intuition. You have streamlined your access to it. If you have a difficult decision to make, I suggest you complete all four steps in this practice and quietly remain in the fourth stage as you ask for guidance and wait to hear an answer from your higher intelligence.

practice 5 *meditate like a mountain*

*Feel more grounded when your mood
is up and down*

Diagnostic

One of the most common problems in our society is the sensation
of feeling up and down on an "emotional rollercoaster." When we
get a new job we "jump for joy," and we have incredible energy. If
we lose our job, we fall down. New spouse? We fly! But if our new
boyfriend or girlfriend leaves us, we fall down. Money problems
follow the same pattern. We receive money, we jump; lose money,
we fall. Day after day, starting in childhood, we have etched this
addiction into our subconscious; we are up and down all the time.
This perpetual movement seems natural to us. We think that life is
just this way, and it seems that there is no other way to live. How
can we learn to avoid the rollercoaster of emotions and find a life
of stability? To feel nothing—to be completely emotionless—would
be impossible and undesirable. Emotions are tools that help us
measure and reflect our thinking. Without emotions we would
have a difficult time registering the pattern of our thoughts.

We experience stress, our emotions move up and down,
our mind is a yo-yo, because we are not present to our lives. If
we want to be more grounded and centered, we must learn to be
present. We must consciously choose to bring stability into our

minds and bodies. The more stable we are, the better we feel, the more easily we work, and the deeper we live.

There is no ocean without waves, no life lived without challenges. We understand in life there are things we cannot escape: losing family members and friends, growing older, health and financial problems, and so forth. This being said, we should not be surprised when these kinds of things happen. The less we are surprised when difficulties emerge, the more stable we feel, and the better prepared we are to handle any challenge that comes our way.

Our capacity to be grounded totally changes the way we choose to live out these moments. Every challenge that is sent to us in this life will either destroy us or become a lesson, an occasion to grow strong in our faith, determination, and inner peace.

When the mind is stable, the body feels good. The relationship between mind and body cannot be overemphasized. A stable energy in the mind boosts the immune system, reducing fatigue and the risk of falling ill. When we are not stable, we are decentered; our emotions act like waves crashing against our inner peace. Stress creates illness, and illness can create more stress. There is no escape from this cycle unless we make a conscious decision to break the pattern. Our ultimate nature, peace, and access to our spiritual dimension depend on this choice.

A clear mind allows positive and intuitive thinking, which allows us to make the best decisions. Good decisions create good outcomes, and good outcomes create positive perceptions. Stability is the first step in this cycle: It opens the way for positive and intuitive thinking, and as we know, our thoughts create our entire experience of life. For many years I have practiced stabilizing the mind. Now, when a challenge arises, I am not thrown off by the surprise that a difficulty has come; rather, my mind can immediately set to work on finding a solution. The stress of difficulties comes from our not anticipating them; by knowing they will come, we save valuable time and energy.

Visualization: Meditate Like a Mountain

Our practice comes straight from Hesychia, a way of meditation taught for centuries at Mount Athos in Greece, in the Eastern Orthodox Christian tradition.

For many centuries and across cultures, spiritual teachers have known the importance of the posture of the mountain. In the Gospel of Matthew, when Jesus delivers the Sermon on the Mount (the beatitudes), he does so at the top of the mountain. When I saw how my rinpoche meditated, I was always surprised by the simplicity of his method: He was just sitting down, but with an incredibly deep presence. No special attitude. He just sat with a posture like a mountain. When my spiritual teacher, theologian Jean-Yves Leloup, went to Mount Athos for the first time and asked how to begin to learn to meditate, the answer from his guru was, "Sit down, but like a mountain."

Perhaps when you first started meditating, your instinct was to go into nature, to the top of a hill or mountain. The vantage point from a mountain has a spiritual association in our mind. Just as we can overlook a city from a high vantage point, we can overlook the circumstances of our lives with distance. In both cases we see the big picture more clearly.

This practice of meditating like a mountain is one of the first I teach in my classes. It is especially easy to teach children. The mountain is the symbol of spiritual life: Its majestic nature—its power and presence—is understood from even an early age. Its stability, certainty, and size remind us that we are part of a planet and a universe much grander than ourselves. This helps us take a step back from the questions and concerns we have about the "outside world" and focus back within, taking a look at our lives from above, similar to the lesson we learned in Practice 2: Meditate Like a Dolphin. From the top of the mountain we see farther, with greater clarity, and with a wider understanding and point of view.

Regardless of religious beliefs, the mountain has been a symbol for introspection and perspective throughout the world. Perhaps in your own experience, you can recall a time that you went hiking up a trail to reach the top of the mountain and saw how your thoughts were quiet and your perspective open.

When we stay at the ordinary level of consciousness, we remain inside our situation, and we can't see past our difficulties. At the top of a mountain, we become more like the mountain and less like our anxious or worried selves.

The goal of this visualization is to become a mountain, wherever we are, right now. I usually suggest this practice for the workplace, because it is easy to do at your desk, particularly when challenges arise.

At first, you may find it helpful to undertake this practice in nature, to engrave in your memory the feeling of peace you are likely to find there. But this practice has been adapted for you to use anytime, anywhere, whether at your desk, riding the subway, on a park bench, or in your bed.

When we practice like a mountain, we gain the weight of

the spiritual presence of the mountain. When we become like a mountain we feel the presence and energy of the mountain, day by day, and the eternity of nature. In theology, we say that we feel the presence of God inside our presence. The divine energy supersedes our human condition.

Guidance

Exercise 1: Discover the Mountain

Before practicing, read this guidance to help with the practice. Just before you read, take a deep breath to show respect for the words, which were written for you.

> Begin just as you are, sitting down,
> at your desk or near your computer, looking at an image
>   of a beautiful mountain.
> Study this mountain.
> Take a few minutes to memorize the image,
> and then close your eyes.
> You are sitting down
> just like the mountain.
> You don't move.
> You do nothing.
> Remain seated, like a mountain.
> You feel the weight of the mountain
> in your spine and back.
> You feel deeply grounded, rooted in the earth.

If you have distracting thoughts in your mind,
>   you do nothing.
Thoughts are like clouds in the sky above your mountain.
A mountain does not move
when there are clouds above it, so you don't move.
You are absolutely still.
Breathe quietly, inhaling for five seconds.
Hold your breath for five seconds,
and exhale for five seconds.
You are still, like a mountain.
You discover that you can sit down without moving,
feel the weight of the mountain hold you firmly to the chair,
as you practice meditating like a mountain.

CLOSE YOUR EYES

~

PRACTICE

~

OPEN YOUR EYES

When we open our eyes, we feel a little calmer. We are aware of the weight and presence of our own bodies; perhaps we even feel heavy. When we don't move our body, we feel more present, quieter. It is amazing to see how a simple practice can affect our minds and bodies so quickly. It is not easy to spend time without moving around, especially if we are anxious and we have running thoughts, so let's practice the second step to help ease into a deeper practice.

Exercise 2: Become a Mountain

Before reading the next guidance, take a deep breath to pay respect to these words.

> You are happy to be sitting down,
>> contemplating your image of a mountain.
> It is easier than the first time
> to be still and remain seated, quietly, looking at
>> your mountain.
> This mountain does not move.
> Your body does not move.
> Your body, your mind, becomes like the mountain.
> Without movement, without agitation.
> Still.
> You feel how it is good to be calm,
> and to see this mountain, deeply.
> If there are noises around you,
> like stray thoughts in your mind,
> you ignore them
> and listen to the wind,
> as the mountain does.
>
> You hold the image of this mountain in your mind
> just before closing your eyes.
> You start to feel the energy of the mountain.
> This sensation is powerful.

The mountain does not move.

The mountain does not think.

The mountain is still.

It is present.

And you are present like the mountain.

You feel how relaxing it is just to be present

and seated like the mountain.

Close your eyes.

Feel the presence of the mountain.

The energy of the mountain.

For many centuries, it has not moved.

It has no time.

It lives in eternity.

Feel its stability.

Deeply.

Feel its stability throughout your body.

Visualize the mountain's energy in your body, in your mind.

The longer you remain seated like a mountain,

the more you become a mountain.

The more you embrace eternity,

the more present you are,

the more stable you are,

the calmer you feel,

the safer you feel.

No stress, no doubt, no tension.

Like a mountain.

CLOSE YOUR EYES

~

PRACTICE

~

OPEN YOUR EYES

In just a matter of seconds, you became a mountain. It was a deep sensation, registered in every cell of your body, in every neuron in your brain. Your muscles are more relaxed. When you opened your eyes, you were surprised to see that you are not in a beautiful landscape, but rather just sitting down in your daily life. You have used your surroundings to create a shrine in your mind, a safe place to escape to and re-center your mind and body; you have found a refuge. Let's now proceed to Exercise 3 to deepen our practice with the mountain.

Exercise 3: The Mountain Is Inside of Us

Before reading the following guidance, take a deep breath to show respect for these words, which are written like a prayer. You will practice with your eyes closed, and you will remember this guidance.

> You are sitting down,
> like a mountain, looking at the image of a mountain.
> And you breathe,
> inhaling and exhaling deeply.
> When you breathe,

you feel the energy of the mountain entering inside of you.
You see how the energy, eternity, and stability
of the mountain
become your own.
When you inhale, you diffuse this energy, eternity,
and stability throughout your body.
You can follow the journey of the mountain's energy
inside you.
You are entering into a relationship with the mountain.
A simple relationship.
You become the mountain.
You feel more stable, calm.
You feel more *mountain*.
You become free like a mountain.
A mountain has no ups and downs,
it just is.
This sensation, to be seated like a mountain,
to feel the energy of the mountain
in your body and mind, is miraculous.
You feel the eternity, the stability, of the mountain.

Now you close your eyes, to feel this sensation more deeply.

CLOSE YOUR EYES

~

PRACTICE

~

OPEN YOUR EYES

How do you feel? You sense stability in your soul. You feel this sensation physically. Also, you feel more confident. When you are more stable, when your mind is less like a yo-yo, you feel more present, which leads you to feel more confident and stronger when you face difficult situations.

Once we are comfortable with this exercise, we can move on to the last level of the practice. We can feel the presence of the universe, a presence grander than ourselves, in our mountain.

Exercise 4: The Presence of the Universe Is Inside Us

Before reading this guidance, take a deep, respectful breath.

> You are seated,
> and immediately you feel connected with your mountain.
> The mountain becomes your friend, your spiritual teacher,
> a structure for your mind and, therefore, your body.
> You feel that inside the mountain there is energy.
> In every mountain there is a divine energy,
> a supreme energy, the energy of the universe.
> In every mountain there are particles of the universe.
> There is a memory of the universe.
> The Presence of the Universe.
> A presence grander than ourselves.
> You can feel the connection
> when a presence grander than yourself
> touches your presence.
> Suddenly you are One.

A bridge between the sky and the earth,
between the Presence of the Universe
and your human presence.
The Presence of God in the human.
The divine in the human.

When you practice deeply, you can feel the stability of the
    universe
become your stability.
You feel the eternity of the universe
in your short practice time.
You are linked to the universe.
You are in another state of consciousness.
You feel a quality of peace that is not human,
but divine.
The divine inside your humanity,
like a mountain inside of you.

CLOSE YOUR EYES

~

PRACTICE

~

OPEN YOUR EYES

It is amazing to feel the power of the energy of the universe inside
you through the mountain visualization.

You are deeply happy. You feel more present. This is not
woo-woo nonsense, but a real experience that you have created

as you became a mountain today. When you practice regularly you will find it easier to be still like a mountain for longer periods of time. When you practice like a mountain, you enjoy more freedom. You expand your reality so you can seek and find solutions to any problem, any difficulty, or any source of stress.

practice **6** *meditate like a wave*

Deal with difficult people and
difficult interactions

Diagnostic

Every day we breathe in mental toxins, stress, sadness, and violence around us. The intrusion of shadow into our light is constant. This process of taking in the bad news of the world is only getting more and more severe. For example, our movies are increasingly violent, news programs include fewer positive stories, and all this negative information comes at us faster than ever. The emotions around us are contagious. We live in a stressful environment with little time to ourselves, so we breathe stress. The more we breathe this negative energy, the more stressed we become. There is no end.

We can't change reality, but we can change our perception of it by recycling it. We can transform the shadows around us into light. We can recycle ignorance into intelligence, stupidity into compassion, and sadness into happiness. We can change our experience of life by changing our perception of it.

I will teach this change through the practice of meditating like a wave, using the *tonglen*, a Tibetan term that I translate roughly as "recycling." (I explain this concept in depth at the back of the book, beginning on page 182.) Practice the wave and you can change your life. Not after one year of practicing, but immediately—after the first time.

The first time I presented this practice to my parolee friends at the Amity Foundation in Los Angeles, it made an impact. Many of my students there have chronic addictions, have taken antidepressants for long periods of time, and fight through a multitude of mental health issues after years spent incarcerated. The moment they practiced the wave, they felt better. Their success made me cry. We all saw how simple it was to feel better immediately. We saw how the world could be better right now if we practice the wave and learn to recycle the shadow into light.

It is the same process for a workplace. What is the goal of a company? To develop more stability, prosperity, and profit. What does a company need to avoid? Bad energy, tension, and overly fatigued employees. A company must create a positive energy and a positive collective mind. Positive ambiance in the workplace fosters happy employees who are creative and intuitive. This is especially true in our competitive global market; products and services can be provided from any part of the world. As all emotions are contagious, more employers need to make the decision to bring positive energy to their workplace, allowing their employees to be inspired, driven, and, most importantly, happy.

What do we need to develop positive energy? No judgment from our coworkers, no negative emotions, no mental toxins. Why is it that so often our work is filled with these destructive attitudes? Because we have never learned the most important teaching about the workplace, to be positive, kind, and altruistic. Some people say that stress, sadness, and anxiety are normal. But we see how those emotions create a bad mood for all who surround us. So it is not "normal," nor is it healthy. It is the opposite of our nature, because our nature is to be kind, calm, and altruistic. Our natural state is to feel good, not off-balance. So how can we recycle the mental toxins, the stress that we encounter every day? As Gandhi said, you must be the change you want to see in the world.

This is a rather urgent matter. If this change does not happen within a few years, surely our economic system will crash. In some studies, up to 80 percent of Americans claim to be close to burning out, at all levels of management. In just a few years, I am sure that everyone will know someone who has fallen ill from work-related stress, and I don't mean a simple cold or flu. Stress is an epidemic, and we need to see that it contributes to killing us. It's really that simple.

We need to recycle the shadows around us. When we do this, we discover that we are not slaves to our mental habits. We can protect ourselves from the emotions of others. We can forgive others when they are not kind or understanding and continue to stand in our own light. We can live every day without tension or problems, because we understand, at a profound level, that in life there are no problems, only situations waiting to be resolved. And in every situation, there is the seed of a solution.

We can practice meditating like a wave at work or at home to recycle the bad energy we receive every day. This is also the practice we can use if we have an addiction, whether it is to drugs or alcohol or to a toxic emotion like jealousy, violence, fear, mental confusion, or chronic dissatisfaction.

Every emotion has a starting point, like a wave on the ocean. With this practice, we learn how to identify the start of the process—the emotion or the addiction. For example, if we have an alcohol addiction, we can practice every day to be ready when the desire to drink starts; when we identify the start of the pattern, it is easier to stop and recycle it.

Visualization: Meditate Like a Wave

Native American tradition says that nature is the book of wisdom. Most of our visualizations come from this idea. Nature is our highest spiritual teacher because it teaches our ego with only pure consciousness. One day, on Santa Monica Beach, I meditated facing the ocean, and I saw how each wave was like each of my thoughts. It was a very clear picture. I saw how a wave started and resolved, just like an emotion. Both the wave and the emotion are part of a larger whole, but each one can be seen, felt, and experienced. This realization inspired me to create this teaching.

When we see a wave, we can mentally visualize the wave flowing through us. We can see how the wave enters us to take out all the stress, the bad emotions that we keep inside our subconscious, and how the wave returns back to its source, carrying these toxins with it. We can feel the force of the wave, the great force of the ocean, as it offers its energy to help you detox and recycle bad emotions and addictions. The ocean is constantly recycling, so we connect with this characteristic to recycle our own fatigue and challenges. I have adapted this practice for use at the workplace.

Before Arriving at Work

We can meditate like a wave before we arrive at the office. We can practice it just after we wake up or during our commute. As we know, prevention is the best medicine, so coming into work with a clear mind and a positive energy can determine how you feel for the entire day. When we practice beforehand, it is easier to be ready when the mental toxins attack us. Prevention is key.

Also, when we practice before work, we realize how recycling difficulties is natural to us. The goal of the wave is to detox, to recycle, but also to wake up our consciousness. We can recycle at any opportunity, anytime, by simply using our breath and mind. We forget that every emotion is a choice, and we can choose when the wave returns to the sea. Practicing teaches us to be more alive, more conscious, and we realize how all is nature inside us.

My friend Dr. Amchi Tsetan (perhaps the most highly regarded practitioner of traditional Tibetan medicine in the world) says that recycling our difficulties throughout the day, many times per day, is the best medicine. We fall ill when we allow these difficulties to latch onto us, and we use our energy and immune system to release them only after they have a hold. The health of the body can be protected and improved using this meditation practice.

During Work

It is of utmost importance to practice while we are at work, to release any bad energy we may receive during the day. Of course, most of the time we keep bad energy for many days, weeks, or even several years. This is the reason we become deeply fatigued and sick. The key to this practice is to become a living example of the visualization, a living wave. In the monastery, they say that the goal of life is to become a living prayer, a living consciousness. All the waves of the ocean are in perpetual movement to teach this lesson to us every minute of our lives.

When we detox, we feel better. We diffuse good energy, and this energy will positively impact our relations with our families, friends, coworkers, and managers. We realize how the world around us depends on the world inside of us, and how we can recycle our difficulties to change the world.

After Work

Of course, when we practice before and during work, we feel lighter leaving work and returning home. Before leaving work, or on our way back home, we can detox and recycle once more. Bad emotions from the day can stay with us like a spiritual virus. Some bad emotions are very deep and aggressive, so we must never underestimate how sensitive we are to these emotions.

Before Going to Sleep

As a society, we suffer from insomnia because we hold onto too many mental toxins and stressful thoughts and emotions. Billions of people suffer from sleep deprivation and take prescription pills that carry undesirable side effects. In my experience, there is no pill that can cure the root of the problem; pills are only temporary fixes for the symptoms of sleep deprivation. When we use pills to "cure" insomnia, we forget that the cause of the insomnia is only growing deeper and deeper in our subconscious, day after day. The root of our problem is in our emotions, which are very sensitive to the energies around us. There are no chemical pills that can recycle bad emotions. You must devote time and effort to curing the energies and emotions that have latched onto you. This will cure the root of the problem and allow you to feel better.

Retreat with the Waves

We will meditate with visualization, but of course it is wonderful if you can practice meditating like a wave with the ocean itself. To smell the ocean, to feel the energy of nature around and inside of you, is incredible medicine and can help you engrave in your mind the practice of recycling bad energy.

For Alcohol and Drug Addictions and PTSD

As mentioned earlier, we can adapt this practice of meditating like a wave to addiction. Every addiction has a very clear process, like a wave. So when we practice we learn how to feel the start of the wave, of the addiction, and by recognizing the start of the craving or need, we are able to control the wave and stop its power over us. Use this practice to create a strict cognitive prevention program; be very diligent to see how your "wave" starts and learn to catch the wave before its current pulls you under.

When we meditate through the start of the addictive feeling (for drugs, alcohol, sex, or anything else), we are more prepared to say "no" when the craving comes back. It can take a lot of practice, but our brain has the capacity to be reprogrammed like a computer.

Guidance

Exercise 1: Feel the Tactile Sensation of Pain

Before practicing, before closing your eyes, read this guidance.
As you prepare to read, take a deep breath to pay respect to
these words, which were written for you.

Begin just as you are, sitting down,
facing your computer,
or wherever life finds you.

Close your eyes,
and feel the many thoughts, stresses, and mental toxins
inside you.
You are at your workplace, and it is difficult.
Today, you have faced judgments or criticism from your
coworkers.
You visualize this stress in your mind, in your body,
in your cells.

With your eyes still closed,
you can feel a tactile sensation of pain.
For example, you can visualize your stomach.
You feel and see a dark color in it.
When you see this, you really feel the pain.
You can feel the movement of the pain,
like a virus moving through the body.

For women, sometimes these mental toxins are registered
     in the genitals.
For men, it can be in the liver, the kidneys, or the prostate.
You can feel the pain.

Listen to your body,
and try to feel where the mental toxins are,
the pain you have received today.
When you inhale,
you see the dark cloud that has formed around your organs.
When you exhale, you see this dark cloud leave with
     the breath.
See it exit your body and enter into the air.
The shadow does not return to you,
it simply floats away.
Repeat this inhalation and exhalation
until the entire cloud is gone,
until there is no dark color left in your body.
You may be able to do this in a few breaths,
or maybe over the course of a few minutes.
Listen to the natural intelligence of your body.

CLOSE YOUR EYES

~

PRACTICE

~

OPEN YOUR EYES

We feel better after we listen to our bodies. Before recycling, we must listen and locate our emotions. Where do you keep your stress? Is it in the mind or the stomach? Listen for your body's answer if you are not sure. When you do this, your pain subsides immediately, because the pain knows that you are listening to it and asking that it leave your body to return to the universe. To listen deeply to your body is the start of the recycling process. We open our minds to an expanding reality and enter a relationship with our pain, our stress.

Most of the time we don't care about healing these difficult emotions. We just complain about them. It is a revelation, a revolution, when our pain feels that we have consideration for it. It is an incredible feeling when we conquer our mental toxins. We have come with the antidote, as the immune system does for the body.

Exercise 2: Discover the Power of the Wave

Before practicing with your eyes closed, read this guidance. As you prepare to read, take a deep breath to respect these words, which are written like a prayer.

> Begin sitting down,
> facing your computer.
> You are looking at a picture of a wave.
> A beautiful, powerful wave.
> You see, you feel, its energy.
> Before closing your eyes,

you love to see the representation of your visualization.
You feel it is helping you
to be more focused, clearer.

With your breath, you can make the sound of the wave.
Breathe deeply, your eyes closed.
And listen to your breath, like the sound of a wave.
If you want to be more focused, breathe louder.
The sound is more accurate.
Listen to the wave inside of you, through your breath.
Now you can breathe the wave and feel it travel inside you.
You feel it deeply flowing through your body.

Breathe with the wave.
See that the wave enters you,
and touches the dark clouds of your bad emotions.
Feel the moment the wave touches your pain.
Hold your breath for three seconds,
then exhale powerfully,
allowing the wave of dark emotion to go back into the sea.
When you exhale, you feel an incredible sensation
as you expel the dark cloud from your body.

Do the practice again to engrave it deeper into the
        subconscious.
Close your eyes,
breathe in as the wave enters you,
touches your pain,

reaches your bad emotions.
Hold your breath for three seconds
and breathe out the darkness inside you.
Liberate your mental toxins,
liberate the suffering inside yourself.

CLOSE YOUR EYES

~

PRACTICE

~

OPEN YOUR EYES

You will feel a sensation of relief that something has been taken out of your mind, your body, your self. It is a clear perception. You are really recycling; you are taking out the mental suffering that you have inside you. It is an amazing moment to live this new perception.

Exercise 3: Offer Your Suffering to the Universe

Before practicing, before closing your eyes, read this guidance. As you prepare to read, take a deep breath to show respect for these words, which are written like a prayer.

You are sitting down,
facing your computer.
You are so happy to practice;
you feel it brings real change to your life.

First you visualize the wave on your computer
or whatever device you have.

You are so happy to breathe with your wave,
to feel how it enters inside you,
and the sound of this wave is made
with the sound of your breath.

You breathe this wave, you inhale,
and the wave enters you.
You hold your breath for three seconds,
and you see that the wave gathers up your pain and
takes it out, far away from you.
When you exhale,
you clearly see that the wave takes away your suffering.
What a freeing sensation to feel this gift,
to feel that you don't hold onto the suffering of others.

Now, practice deeper.
You see the wave enter inside you.
Hold your breath for three seconds,
and with all of the force of the wave,
exhale,
liberate the bad emotion,
liberate the person suffering inside yourself,
and offer this breath to the universe.
With your eyes firmly closed, it is easier.
You offer your suffering to the sky.

You are recycling the dark into light.
In the universe, the bad emotion is dissolving.
Forever and ever.
You watch as the darkness
travels into the sky,
and transforms into a beautiful, pure white light.

CLOSE YOUR EYES

~

PRACTICE

~

OPEN YOUR EYES

You are calmer, freer. You are recycling your difficulties, but more than that, you are offering your difficulties to the light. All darkness is transformed. You realize that you can have this very concrete sensation at work, at home, or anywhere you encounter difficult energies. You see that when you intentionally push the darkness outside of yourself, you live with a new perception of your emotions. You are the master of your universe, of your experience.

Exercise 4: Love Your Pain

Before practicing and closing your eyes, read this guidance. As you prepare to read, take a deep breath to show respect for these words.

You are sitting down,
facing your computer,
and you watch the wave on your screen.

Breathe in your wave,
and hold the breath for three seconds.
See how exhaling
forces out the dark cloud of your mental toxins.

Offer this darkness to the light of the universe.
The more you practice like this,
the more you feel your pain is reduced, breath after breath.

And you can experience an incredibly high level of
        compassion.
You can say thank you to the pain you've endured.
Thank you for pushing me to meditate.
Because without you, I would have never practiced the wave.
Because without you, I would never feel better.
My pain, I love you, because you stimulate me.
Every day, you train me in my determination.
Every day, you train my intelligence.

And I feel an incredible joy to liberate you,
to remove you from my body,
from my soul,
from every cell.

Every day, I rediscover how it is possible to recycle you,
to cure me, to become more present to my life,
more intelligent in my life,
more compassionate,
as I offer you to the universe.
Thank you for teaching me that I can be free.
Thank you for teaching me how I can help my coworkers,
managers, friends, and family every day.
Thank you for teaching me to be vigilant in my meditation.

Thank you to my pain, my mental toxins, my stress,
for becoming my spiritual teachers.
Forever and ever.

Thank you to my alcohol addiction
for becoming my spiritual teacher.
Thank you to my drug addiction
for becoming my spiritual teacher.
Thank you to my PTSD,
for becoming my spiritual teacher.
Forever and ever.

Thank you to
all the bad emotions, the traumas
that I have experienced in my life.
You have taught me how to recycle,
how to liberate you from my body,
from my soul,

from my every cell.
Today, facing my computer,
with the practice of the wave,
I have rediscovered the purpose of my life.

Thank you to my pain for having saved my life,
for teaching me the value of my well-being.
Through a simple wave.
The wave of my life.

You are born to become waves.
You are waves.

CLOSE YOUR EYES

~

PRACTICE

~

OPEN YOUR EYES

As a parent takes care of a child, self-nurturing is part of our nature.
We know this because it makes us feel well. We have the capacity
to recycle and liberate our bad emotions, and we see how easy it is
to arrive at this state of awareness if we just practice the wave.

practice *7* _meditate like the sun_

Restore energy, send all your love to others,
and discover the power of compassion

Diagnostic

We are easily stressed because we are tired. We are tired because we are stressed. It is a vicious circle, with no end.

Physical fatigue

We are exhausted when we take the subway, drive in traffic, or otherwise travel to work every day, carrying our many bags with us. Every day our body is tired and rarely given adequate time to recharge. When we do have free time, it is rarely free: Our minds are occupied day and night, twenty-four hours per day. Even in our sleep, the subconscious is hard at work, often more so than during the day. So our muscles, our cells, our organs are tired. And when we have the chance to exercise, we feel better, but a few hours later, or the day after, we are tired again. Sometimes, we have the chance to go on vacation over a weekend. We love that. It is a wonderful moment. But we know the truth. When we come back to our daily life, we will be tired, more and more, day after day.

According to Tibetan medicine, we are tired because the fire element is out of balance in our body. We are not warm enough, we are too cold, and our water element is dominant.

Psychological fatigue

Every day our mind learns, remembers, and thinks about millions of pieces of information and data. We say that our brain is like a computer. But when our brain crashes, there is no back-up drive. Our brain is not a computer. Our brain is our body, and most times, we don't take care of it. We don't pay any attention to our mind's fatigue, mostly because we have had no teaching to do so. We are not educated on how our minds are the key to our lives, our bodies, our destinies.

So day after day, we have psychological fatigue, and we think that it is normal. We take pills to sleep, or antidepressants to help our moods, but we know in our hearts that this medicine cannot fix the root of our problems. We are deeply and psychologically exhausted, and we fear the future has no solutions to alleviate us. We feel tired physically when we are tired psychologically. It is a vicious circle.

We have no energy to meditate. Sometimes we read a book about spirituality or go to a conference, but it is like a spiritual Band-Aid, because nothing really changes inside of us. We fight chronic fatigue until our body says, "No, I refuse to accept this fatigue, and I will make you aware of this through illness." Many times, when this illness starts, it can be too late to stop, or it takes a long time to make the right changes in our lives to restore healthy living.

Spiritual or essential fatigue

There is a sort of fatigue deeper than the physical or psychological, a fatigue that is far more vicious: spiritual, or essential, fatigue.

The fatigue of the nonsense in our lives. Why do we overwork for our company, even when we are not happy? Why have we become zombies? Where is the sense in this kind of life? Day after day, this type of fatigue is deeply painful. And we have no solution, because if we lost our job, it would be worse. What can we do? How can we escape from this jail?

In theology, we say we feel spiritual fatigue because we are far from the divine energy, far from God. But when we must work fifteen hours each day, with just a few days every year for vacation, how can we talk about spirituality, about theology? It is not possible.

In Buddhism, we say that if we don't practice every day, if we don't read teachings and go on retreats, we can't open our consciousness to other perspectives. And if we are broken physically, psychologically, and spiritually, how will we survive?

One day, I was teaching a class to college students in New York, and a young Chinese student came to me at the end of my teaching and explained that he wanted to kill himself. He saw how his life, lived without awareness, was depressing and absurd. His parents in China worked overtime to pay his tuition, which made him feel guilty. And he explained that after his studies he would have to continue making payments for many years, working a job with a high level of stress. He was broken, and he felt that there was no hope. But the meditation workshop had made him cry, and he said that the awareness he gained had given him hope. He ultimately chose not to commit suicide.

When the three types of fatigue break us, we activate the depression region in the brain. It is painful to have to live this way.

The secret of good energy

How can we escape? How can we find a new type of energy, immediately?

We can take pills. The pills try to cure the symptoms of fatigue, not the root of the problem. We know this is true because we are tired again a few hours or a few days later. And the more we get high artificially—through drugs, alcohol, addictions, shopping, sex, and ego—the more seriously we crash later on. What can we do to feel better, more positive, more active, and happier?

I could tell you that you must learn to meditate, and practice every day for thirty minutes, but this is a fantasy for most people. We are too tired, and we have no time for that. So what is the answer?

The power of a little attention

We must reactivate our heart, our fire element. When we are exhausted, we need a little attention. We need to reactivate a special energy from our heart, from the source of our life, from the sun in the cosmology of our bodies. We escape. We break the wall of our egos, of our closed-minded attitudes. Suddenly our heart explodes, like a sun. We enter a new, altruistic cycle of energy.

Our human nature is to be like the sun, a great fire. If we become more like it, we restore our energy and become more helpful, because we become who we are at our core.

The power of a little attention can change your life, in one second.

For example, you are exhausted in the subway, but suddenly someone faints and you help this person. You take her in your arms and give her your seat. This person feels better and sends a wonderful message in her smile that says, "Thank you, from my heart." You immediately feel a warm energy inside of you. At the moment when you return the smile, you activate more than fifty muscles in your face. You immediately send a powerful, positive message to your cells, from your cortex.

When you see a child crying in the street you stop and talk to him. He feels listened to. You feel how you have helped him. Maybe his family does not give him enough attention. You feel how your altruistic gesture has helped both of you, and the energy from a gesture like this is nothing short of contagious.

Your wife comes home, exhausted. You are preparing a beautiful bath with incense and candles. She is so surprised and happy. It diffuses happiness in your home, leaving everyone less stressed and brighter.

Your manager does not feel well, so you go to the coffee shop and bring him a warm tea. He smiles at you. It brings good energy to your desk, something magical and positive, like perfume. Suddenly, you discover that beyond this job, your manager is human, and it is a miracle to be alive, to see our coworkers and managers every day.

At work, a coworker discovers that she has cancer, and you talk to her with all your heart, and you take her hand. You feel how helpful it is to really listen—without ego—to someone in great suffering. You feel how at this moment your help and attitude are a pure gift of compassion.

Sometimes you are broken by fatigue, but you go home and see your dog. She is waiting for you by the door. You take her to the dog park and watch as she jumps around, appreciating her life. You take her in your arms. It is a deep feeling, to love your pet.

You feel better, without effort. No teaching, no meditation, just reactivating your heart energy through compassion and altruism. Your heart becomes the sun.

There is no feeling more powerful than when we are helpful. During these moments, our minds enter another state of consciousness. We are driven not by egotism, but by altruism. Neuroscience tells us that these actions develop the region of our brain associated with joy. This is a great remedy for depression and anxiety. Our body feels this sensation immediately and in a very real and tangible way.

Of course, when we are tired we must recycle our fatigue to reactivate our spiritual energy. Have you ever felt tired after giving or receiving a compassionate gesture? It is unlikely. The body naturally regenerates its energy when it feels these emotions. It is the easiest way to restore spiritual energy. Nothing is more powerful and beautiful than the power of a little attention.

Visualization: Meditate Like the Sun

The sun is a very well-known symbol in spiritual traditions. In the Hesychia orthodox tradition, they say, "meditate like a sunflower," because our hearts are oriented to the sun. When we meditate like the sun, we reactivate our energy with the sun. We become lighter, brighter, and we transmit all our light and fire energy to ourselves and all those around us.

According to shamanic tradition, both in Buddhism and Native American cultures, our heart is like the sun. Our organs are like planets in the cosmos of our bodies. The sun is the heart of the solar system, just as our heart is the center of our body.

In Tibetan medicine, we say that any little altruistic gesture or attitude reactivates our fire element. Meditating like the sun means using this mental picture to stimulate our source of energy and sending this bright energy to others, like rays from the sun.

We will use also this meditation like fire to diffuse good energy throughout our body. We know the incredible power that connects our minds and our cells, muscles, and organs. Even at work we can use our heart like a fire and diffuse energy into our tired muscles.

The neuroscientist Dr. Mario Beauregard is trying to prove the medical benefits of compassion. He believes it is possible to prove that when we diffuse altruistic energy we modify our temperature, our immune system, and our environment.

So let us meditate like the sun, at our desk.

Exercise 1: Heart Like the Sun

At our workplace, we can give attention—a small gesture—to someone in need. It can be as simple as a phone call, a cup of tea, a compliment, or careful listening.

Before practicing with closed eyes, take a deep, respectful breath and read this guidance.

You are sitting down,
facing your computer.
On the screen there is an image of the sun.
It is so beautiful.
Looking at this picture will help you visualize.

Your heart is like the sun you see on the computer.

Your heart is a sun in your body.

It beats like a sun.

It has the form of a sun.

There is a sun at the center of your body.

Just as the sun sends its warm energy,

your heart diffuses its love in your body.

Every organ can feel the energy of this love.

You can see the orange color of the sun in your mind,

radiating from your heart,

diffused throughout your body.

When you are stressed or tired,

visualizing the love from your heart like a sun energizes you.

You can visualize how your heart is so kind,

so warm, and feel it with every one of your organs—

your arms, your fingers, your legs, your feet.

To see the orange color of the sun,

the pure love in your body, helps you immediately.

Now you can breathe the energy of your heart like a sun.

You feel the dilatation of your heart, like a sun.

You keep this incredible power for just a few seconds

and you enjoy it when you breathe it out

and diffuse it—this beautiful warm energy—throughout your body.

You see that every cell of your body is brighter,

more vivid, happier.

You feel a new energy immediately.

CLOSE YOUR EYES

~

PRACTICE

~

OPEN YOUR EYES

It is a very special sensation. You feel your heart for the first time. Every day when we breathe without awareness, we don't take notice of our first vital organ. To visualize your heart is to see a beautiful sun. When we are tired, we see the dark energy inside us. During these times we realize the power of a mental picture and how it can change our lives. We send the bright orange color of the sun throughout our body to cast out the shadow. We begin to meditate deeper and find a brighter light in our lives.

With this exercise we pay important attention to our body. It will teach us how to help an organ that is sick, say, the liver. When we send mental rays of sun to this organ, we visualize it for a few minutes until the shadow has left this body part. This practice is also a very powerful way to develop a language to communicate with our bodies, with every organ.

Exercise 2: Offer Your Sun at Work

Before practicing with closed eyes, read this guidance to help your practice. As you prepare to read, take a deep breath to show respect for these words.

You are sitting down,
facing the sun on your computer.
You see its rays, orange and yellow, beautifully cast.
Ever since childhood you have loved to see the sun.
To look at this picture of the sun,
to breathe its energy,
brightens your mind immediately.

Breathe in the sun's energy,
hold it for three seconds,
and diffuse its orange color throughout your body.
Breathe in this energy
and your heart becomes a sun.

When you breathe in, you see the sun's rays of light enter
        your heart.
When you breathe out, you diffuse this wonderful light all
        around you,
to everyone at your workplace.
You see the diffusion of this energy,
this orange color, the rays,
and mysteriously you feel warmer, less tired,
and a greater fire within yourself.

It is a wonderful sensation to feel that you can be helpful,
that you can diffuse your sun, your good energy,
to change the environment at your workplace.

All around you, you see your tired coworkers and managers.

You focus your attention on one person.

A coworker, for example.

A coworker you appreciate.

He is tired, very tired.

Why?

Because he never breathes with intention.

He does not care to know his heart.

He does not know that he has the sun within himself.

And with his heart,

he has the power to reactivate his energy when he is tired.

So in silence, deep inside of you, very discretely,

without telling your coworker,

breathe in

and feel your heart beating more deeply,

the sun getting brighter.

Hold your breath for three seconds to feel this energy deep
        inside of you,

and when you exhale diffuse a deep, wonderful energy
        around your coworker

like a ray of light.

Your coworker may or may not see you,

but he feels good energy around and inside of him,

even if he doesn't understand why.

You want to activate more of this energy, to

send this healing light to others around you.

Practice again.

CLOSE YOUR EYES

~

PRACTICE

~

OPEN YOUR EYES

Every day, we spend eight or ten hours, maybe more, with our coworkers. The better our relations with them, the more we share good energy, the better we will feel at work and the easier we will recycle our fatigue. What is worse than having no sense of purpose in life? Forgetting that we have a heart, a sun inside us.

Love is the first energy in nature and the universe. When we damage our link with love and its divine energy, we are lost, sad, and tired. We miss something that we don't understand. We have forgotten our nature.

Exercise 3: Offer Your Sun to Someone You Miss

Before closing your eyes, read this guidance to help your practice. As you prepare to read, take a deep breath to show respect for these words.

You are sitting down,
facing the sun on your computer.
This sun is your heart,
and from a distance you can send rays of light
to others around you.

You have sent your good, warm energy to your organs, to
        your muscles,
and to your coworkers.
Now you can expand the circle.

You are at work, tired, and trying to send your love,
the perfume from your heart,
to someone far from you.
It helps you to be less preoccupied by your job, your daily
        stress, your ego,
and to be more focused on altruism, a greater emotion.

You can look at a picture of a family member or a friend.
It can be someone who has passed on, now in the sky.
At the moment you see this picture on your computer
or cell phone,
you forget your daily stress.
It stimulates your good energy, your heart,
your sun, your fire element, your love.

Just one moment of seeing this person modifies your mind.

You see a person you miss.
You love this person.
So you close your eyes, you breathe deeply,
and you can feel that you have a clearer picture of your heart,
like the sun.

Feel the orange color of your love and its infinitude.

Inhale and hold the breath for three seconds.

Before exhaling, send your loving light to this person.

When you exhale, you diffuse your good energy all around
this person.

Feel how your heart is so close to this person.

You want to feel this wonderful sensation more deeply.

Practice again, deeper and deeper.

Reactivate your relationship with this person.

It is a gift to send your energy to someone you miss.

You feel less alone at work.

You feel more helpful.

You rebuild your confidence.

You are not only a worker, but a human,

who has the genius capacity to reactivate the energy of love.

CLOSE YOUR EYES

~

PRACTICE

~

OPEN YOUR EYES

Practice after practice, our love for our workplace grows. It becomes our shrine, our place to pray. We have a new appreciation of our desk. It is not a stupid place, void of energy and the cause of stress, but a real place to practice. What does this mean? It's a place to be more helpful, more alive. It's a place to live the energy of love.

This energy is like oxygen, flowing all the time, and we can feel the energy of love anywhere. If you are mourning the loss of a loved one, this practice can help you feel reconnected. By sending your loving energy out into the universe, loving energy is returned to you. It is the law of cause and effect, even when the recipient of the energy has made their transition. After all, energy never dies.

Exercise 4: Offer Your Sun to Someone You Usually Don't Appreciate

It is easy to send our pure energy throughout our bodies to a favorite coworker or to a person we miss. But it can be far less easy to send pure love and rays of light to someone we usually don't like. Why is this difficult? What is the goal of a practice like this?

We have seen that when we are tired, not only physically or psychologically but also spiritually, paying attention to another person changes our mind immediately. We are happier and we feel our energy restored.

When we send good energy out to our coworkers, we feel how they are happier, even if they don't understand why. When we practice for someone we miss, we don't see the result. This is because we are sending our energy into the universe without expecting anything back. It is a very spiritual experience to send energy into the universe without the expectation of immediate reward, to send energy just for the sake of sending it.

But when we send our rays of light to someone who does not appreciate us, or to someone we don't appreciate, we enter into the highest level of compassion. We attain the most powerful energy of love, the grandest love of all: divine love. We recycle our fatigue with divine energy.

Before practicing with your eyes closed, read this guidance. As you prepare to read, take a deep breath to show respect for these words.

You are sitting down,
facing the sun on your computer.
Close your eyes,
and visualize someone you don't appreciate
and who does not appreciate you.
Concentrate on this person.
Remember a difficult situation.
The last time he or she was unkind to you.
The last time you were unkind.
Take a deep moment to think about this situation,
      this person.

Take a huge breath, as deep as you can,
from your heart like a sun.
Feel the energy of your heart, so pure, so alive.
You may be close to crying.
Breathe out, deeply, from all your heart, from your sun,
sending pure energy to this person,
beyond your judgments, beyond your misunderstandings,
beyond all the difficult situations.
You may feel that you are traveling through different states
      of mind

and crossing the ordinary level of consciousness.
Send your loving energy to heal this relationship.
It is a miracle. You are flying, mentally.
See that this person is like you.
Not perfect.
He or she, like you, acts with bad judgment many times.
But it is not who you are.
You realize how life is precious, wonderful.
You feel your heart healing.
You feel his or her heart healing.
You realize how simple it is to practice,
to enter into this level of consciousness,
of invincible compassion.
Forever and ever.

CLOSE YOUR EYES

~

PRACTICE

~

OPEN YOUR EYES

Our fire energy heals us and everything in our universe. When we act with compassion, especially at this level, for someone we don't appreciate most of the time, we enter into deep interior freedom. This is the highest practice we can do to restore incredible energy to our lives every day. This is the miracle of life, beyond all challenges that come our way.

practice **8** *meditate like a flower*

Rediscover the blessing of your desk

Diagnostic

When we arrive at work each morning, we sit down at our desks, start our computers, and use our cell phones and iPads, but we don't give much thought to our tools.

The process of sitting down and putting our hands on our electronics comes as second nature to us. We do this without thinking. The manner in which we start our day conditions how the rest of the day goes, so it is to be expected that with this kind of start, the rest of the day will also be without consciousness or presence. As a musician warms up for a performance, so should we tune up our consciousness for the day. But reaching all the way back to childhood, no one has explained to us why it is so important to have a good, proper start to the day.

The same goes for love. When we fall in love with someone, the first few moments, weeks, and months are very important because they set the mood and give direction to the relationship. The perception we have of our lover, formed at the very beginning, becomes deeply imprinted into our subconscious mind. That loving perception will help get us through the tough times we encounter. It will be very helpful in transforming our thoughts and reframing our minds in any hard situation.

Of course, the outcomes of our relationships do not depend only on a good start. A love story can start wonderfully, yet eventually become very difficult. In the same way, a day can start without presence and awareness, but if we receive good news, the day can be totally transformed.

At work, just like in our love life, we are bound to face problems. There is no perfect love, and there is no perfect workday. And just as in life, we will be tired and sick at times, and one day we will be old. We will experience the death of a friend, of a family member, and even our own death. There is no ocean without the waves. There is no life without waves of difficulty. Sometimes, there are even tsunamis.

So what can we do? We can be more prepared before sailing on the ocean of the life. We can start our day mindfully and face our relationships with our eyes open. When problems arise, we will not be caught off guard.

At our desks, there is an energy field. This energy depends on our own personal energy. If we are stressed, we transmit that energy. Every place has an energy. For example, when we arrive in a house where there is tension and people scream all the time, intuitively we feel uncomfortable. When we go to historical sites where very sad events occurred, like the National September 11 Memorial and Museum in New York, we feel deep emotions. These are not merely our thought projections, but concrete feelings embedded in place.

The same is true at our offices. If we start our day without paying attention, if we let stress grow day by day, we keep our lives down with low energy. It does not make our work easier or make us more inspired. It does not help to recycle and transform the mental toxins we receive. The energy of our workplace is exactly like that of a person—stressed out and tired, more and more every day.

We understand that it is important to work in a stress-free environment. So what do some companies do? They implement nice decor or build a restaurant inside the workplace. But they are focused only on appearances. It doesn't work. I know many big companies that have invested a lot of money in the environment of their workers, but in reality the workers are still very stressed. Of course it is good to create a nice working environment, but it is not enough. To cure the symptoms and consequences of our lack of awareness is one thing, but to cure the roots of our unconsciousness is another thing altogether.

What can we do every morning when we arrive at work? How can we stimulate and reawaken our consciousness? How can we rediscover our desk, to see it with new, open eyes? How can we be more vigilant, more aware?

In a monastery we start our day by blessing our surroundings. With incense, songs, prayers, and purification rituals, we rediscover and celebrate the space around us. Subconsciously we create a deep connection to our place. To give this kind of attention to a place is to bless the life in it. We don't take our surroundings for granted; we treat them with respect.

Of course, many monks and nuns do not fully concentrate when they pray. And it is not simply because we go through a ritual to purify a monastery that we are made pure. Sometimes what we actually go through is just an empty mental habit. The quality of our blessing depends on our motivation.

If we bless the monastery, we train our minds to be more awake. Just like every morning, when we bless our lover with a kiss from our heart and we prepare breakfast with love, we give them incredible respect and a blessing, and we help them have a good start to their day.

The point is not to treat our desk like a monastery or to bring religious concepts to work. It is to rediscover and appreciate, to offer good energy—a respectful energy—to our desk every morning.

Visualization: Meditate Like a Flower

Flowers are powerful symbols in many religions.

For example, the rose is the symbol of our heart. It has the same form and the same color. Saint Therese of Lisieux used this symbol to describe her heart, and said, "I will send you a shower of roses, from the sky." In many situations, people have observed the scent of a rose as the signature of the presence of Saint Therese. Mother Teresa also used the rose to talk to people broken by life. She was called Teresa in memory of Therese of Lisieux.

In the Orthodox tradition, Angelus Silesius said, "I want to love like a rose, without reason, just like a rose." In India, the spiritual leader Amma diffuses her love like a rose to everyone she embraces in her arms. In Native American cultures, they use a lot of sage and lavender because their properties are known to purify the energies.

In a monastery we use a lot of incense, like cedar, for example. Why is this practice observed? We do not have enough words to explain what we feel, so we burn plants and flowers to celebrate and to be grateful. The idea is to give honor through incredible energy, respect, and a blessing. It is to reawaken our consciousness of the present moment.

Meditating like a flower is to celebrate and rediscover, to bless our workplace, our desk, and our life without taking anything for granted.

Of course, this does not mean we suddenly arrive at our desk one morning, dressed like a monk—with the bowl haircut, ringing bells, and burning incense—saying, "My dearest coworkers, let me spread the blessing of incense in our workplace and dance, because today we become spiritual forever."

We can't use incense at work, but we can use the visualization of a scent. For these practices, we will use the power of this mental picture, along with our hands.

Guidance

Exercise 1: Breathe the Energy of a Flower

This exercise helps us to rediscover that we have energy, like a perfume, that we can diffuse.

Please download a beautiful picture of your favorite flower. It can be a rose, a lily, or any other flower. We often devote great love and effort to finding the most beautiful flowers.

Before practicing with your eyes closed, read this guidance. As you prepare to read, take a deep breath with respect for these words.

Begin just as you are, sitting down,

facing your computer.

Look at a picture of a flower

that you really admire.

You see that this flower is alive.

You enter into a relationship in your mind with this flower.

See this picture while you breathe in.

Breathe the flower's energy, its perfume.

Your flower becomes more than an object.

You respect its beauty,

its energy, its presence.

With your imagination, you can smell its perfume.

Close your eyes, breathe in the energy of your soul,

the energy of your flower. Hold your breath for

    three seconds,

then breathe out and diffuse it throughout

    your entire body.

The perfume and the energy of this flower are inside you.

Practice again.

See your flower, breathe in the energy,

hold your breath, the energy, the perfume,

and breathe out,

diffusing the energy inside you.

You can visualize the movement of this energy inside you.

You feel the energy inside you, a very real sensation.

CLOSE YOUR EYES

~

PRACTICE

~

OPEN YOUR EYES

For the first time, you feel the energy of this visualization in your body and your mind. You discover that you can breathe in the energy of a flower. We are what we think, what we breathe, what we visualize. So if we see a flower in our minds, if we breathe it in, we are expanding our usual perceptions immediately. We discover that we can breathe in the perfume, the energy of a flower.

Now it's time to go deeper with the practice.

Exercise 2: Bless Your Computer with the Energy of a Flower

Most of the time, we start our computer without even thinking about it. We are on autopilot and have no consideration for this tool. But our computer is incredibly important to us. Naturally, we don't consider or treat our computer like a person; however, we should send this machine good energy. Everything has energy. Doing this is also a way to bless and rediscover our computer, as well as to bless and rediscover our workplace.

Before closing your eyes to practice, read this guidance, taking a deep breath to show your respect for these words.

Begin just as you are, sitting down,
facing your computer.
Visualize that your heart is like a flower.
Mentally diffuse the perfume from your flower to your
computer.

See the perfume of the flower,
the good energy of the flower,
the properties of the flower, flowing out to your computer,
to purify all the messages.

This energy blesses your computer,
to purify all the bad messages we have received.
Every day your computer receives hundreds and hundreds
of emails and messages filled with stress.
All of that energy stays within it.
When you bless your computer with the imagined scent of
a flower, you purify
and mentally reprogram your applications.
You rediscover your computer.

Now breathe deeply,
hold the breath for three seconds,
and exhale while your hands touch your computer.
Feel the contact between your hands and the computer.
Feel the energy from your visualization entering your
computer.
You are blessing your computer.

CLOSE YOUR EYES

~

PRACTICE

~

OPEN YOUR EYES

For the first time, you are aware of your hands on the computer. With the same care and respect you would show while holding a sacred artifact, you can send your computer good energy. You have a new reverence for your computer every morning when you start it. The more respect and consideration you show to your computer, the more you respect your work. The calmer you are, the better prepared you are for the day. Taking care of your computer and of the objects that you use daily is like taking care of yourself.

Your computer is an extension of your life. There is no separation. Everything is connected and interdependent. When you follow this exercise with your computer, you change your perception of the computer. It is no longer an object of stress but a way to become more present. Your computer can become your spiritual teacher every morning. When you see that your heart-flower is opening just like your desktop, it is a blessing.

Exercise 3: Transmit the Energy of the Flower into Your Cell Phone

Every day, we live inside of our cell phones. They are like an extension of our brains, a new appendage. We use them all the time and do almost everything with them. Every day we transfuse our energy to our phones. The more stressed we are, the more we send this little machine stressful energy, and the more we consider it a stressful object.

It is possible to consider our cell phone a great blessing. Every day when we reach for our phone and sense the visualization of the flower inside, we can bless it. By creating an environment of peace and calm around and inside ourselves and in our devices, we generate a healthier perception of our lives. Our cell phones are no longer stress-inducing objects; they represent opportunities to be more present.

Before closing your eyes to practice, read this guidance, taking a deep breath to show your respect for these words.

> Begin just as you are, sitting down,
> facing your cell phone.
> It is on your table, or on your desk.
> Before you turn it on, take one minute to really see it.
> Through it, so many people, so many minds, will talk to you
>   and send their energies.
> Your cell phone is precious; it is your link to the world.
>
> Visualize that your heart is like a flower.
> In your mind's eye you diffuse the perfume of your flower to
>   your cell phone.
>
> Breathe deeply for five seconds.
> At the same time, activate the mental picture of your heart,
>   emitting perfume like a flower.

Hold this perfume, this energy, inside you.

As you exhale, you liberate this energy, this perfume,

in the direction of your cell phone.

Visualize that this perfume enters your cell phone and purifies
all the conversations you had yesterday.

Breathe in again, deeply, while you visualize your heart like a
flower, ready to diffuse perfume with pure energy.

Hold the breath for three seconds

and touch your cell phone with the tips of your fingers.

You see the energy from your heart-flower like perfume
entering your cell phone

to purify and bless every voice, every person, and every soul
who will use this cell phone as a channel to talk to you.

You bless your cell phone.

CLOSE YOUR EYES

~

PRACTICE

~

OPEN YOUR EYES

All is sacred, all is channeled through energy movement. A cell
phone is the channel we use nonstop every day. It is very important
to purify it, as it is our primary form of communication. We
rediscover how to consider it as more than just a simple machine,
as a real tool for channeling positive energy. Spirituality can be
found inside our cell phones. To bless our cell phone is also a very
good form of detoxification, a purification to recycle and transform
all the stress energy we receive every day.

To use our everyday objects, like cell phones, in a different and sacred way is an opportunity to practice becoming more present in our lives. The more we practice in this way, the better prepared we are to face our day. We become more present and more alive. It is easier to keep our minds clear, easier to work, and easier to feel happiness and peace.

Yes, our cell phones, once blessed, can become our spiritual teachers. It is a miracle when we realize, suddenly, that everything and everyone can be blessed, because life is a perpetual blessing.

Exercise 4: Transmit the Energy of the Flower to Your Desk

Just as we arrive at our workplace and bless our computers and cell phones, we can bless our desks. Our desks are usually made of wood, a product of nature. To bless our desk is to reactivate our relationship with this element of the earth.

Before closing your eyes, read this guidance to help with the practice, taking a deep breath to show respect for the words, which were written for you.

You are sitting down,
facing your desk.
Seated like a mountain, you don't move.
Before putting your hands on the desk,
breathe deeply and open your heart like a flower.
Activate the mental perfume of your soul,
the divine energy inside you.

Close your eyes, hold your breath,
and exhale while you touch your desk for the first time today.
Touch it very delicately.
Feel the movement of the energy from your heart-flower,
blooming like a stained glass–rose window onto your desk.
The desk is made of wood.
When your hands touch the desk, when your perfume and
your good energy from your heart-flower touch the
desk through your fingers, you feel contact with
the tree inside of your desk.
You rediscover your desk, not as an inanimate object,
but as the link you have with nature at your workplace.

Breathe again, hold your breath, and enjoy exhaling and
diffusing your energy,
your perfume, to bless your desk when you touch it, just
with the tips of your fingers.

You can say to the desk:
You, dearest tree that lives inside this desk,
I rediscover you,
I have respect and consideration for you;
I am not blind to you.
And when I am stressed, I will breathe deeply
and visualize that my energy, like the perfume of a flower,
comes in contact with the memory of my desk, made of
wood.
I think less, I am more present, I am more grounded.

To bless my desk, to meditate like a flower
that blesses with its perfume, is a miracle.
The beauty of tactile sensation,
the poetic visualization,
and the real sensation of blessing my surroundings—all of
these are miracles.

CLOSE YOUR EYES

~

PRACTICE

~

OPEN YOUR EYES

Our workplace is blessed. Our computers, our cell phones, and
our desks are all blessed. We immediately feel calmer. We have
not lost time in our schedule. More than that, we engrave into our
subconscious day after day the idea that we can find peace. We
can feel the sacred energy at work. We rediscover that peace is like
oxygen, available to us anytime, anywhere. Our perception of life
changes; we break the cliché of peace waiting for us just beyond
the stress. We see how simple it is to be more present. We feel how
easy it is to be more grounded and more positive at work. There is
nothing more beautiful than to bless our workplace each morning,
to rediscover the little things in our daily life, and to celebrate how
this new day is an incredible opportunity to be more alive.

Feel less stress in a romantic relationship

Diagnostic

During difficult times, our romantic partner becomes the most important force in our life. He or she is our refuge and our rock. We can have problems with our coworkers, managers, family, and friends, but the moment we think about our partner, we immediately feel better. We have more energy and more determination. Love is the most powerful energy to transform and change everything. Love is the highest daily teaching of our life.

But then again, our romantic relationships also create a lot of stress. Why is that? Beyond the usual psychological, financial, or sexual intimacy reasons, why do most couples end up separated or divorced due to dissatisfaction? Why are loving relationships so difficult? What is the ultimate reason for this trial, this teaching? Why is it so stressful?

The matter of love and relationships, a subject I love to address in my teaching, could fill the pages of another book.

How can our problems in love become our spiritual teachers?

Normally, when we love someone, we love them for ourselves. This is why we often say, "I need you." I love you, yes, but for selfish reasons. I am not present for you, but only for my projections. I am present for my own needs: my fear of being alone, my trauma from the past, whatever I need, I project onto you. By doing this, we keep ourselves at the level of egotistical love. But egotism is not love. It just creates stress. This kind of "love" leaves us off-centered and unbalanced. We spend a huge amount of energy trying to chase someone to fill that missing need within us, and it is all for nothing, because no one likes to be caught and trapped. So what do we do? We decide to stop and break up with this person, because they can't become the image we decided we needed.

When we project our vision onto the other person, we don't see the real person behind our projection. We see them through a filter. Every day we spend with this person, we go through our usual conversation about jobs, new bosses, money, favorite restaurants, movies, celebrities, political leaders—topics that are merely superficial. We have no real spiritual exchange with them, no essential level of connection. These ordinary shallow interactions cause us stress in the long run. When the stress becomes significant, we usually end things with them. When this happens, it can be more stressful and more painful than before. We become depressed.

After our separation, we try to find someone else, but we reproduce the same archetype, the same "I love you for me" scenario. Again we become stressed, and our lover is not helpful, because this is not altruism; it is egotism. We are trapped in our own mental prison. On this path, there is no hope. We will continue to feel alone.

In theology, we say that when there is no God between two people, the relationship is empty. It is not sacred. It is profane.

There is a spiritual exchange missing. We are trapped in our small world, a shallow perception of life. So we choke. There is no space, no freedom.

When we are at this level of love, we don't really love. We only feed our need not to be alone. It is so painful. We are stuck at a surface level of consciousness, and we are stressed. Year after year, our relationships remain stressful, and we have built nothing. We are not present in our life. Whether it's at the workplace or in our daily relationships, it's the same scenario. We are stressed. We are tired and in mental confusion.

We are in the ego of seduction. We spend a lot of energy trying to chase people. It is a consummation, an infernal consummation. In this state, there is no hope.

Love is not a consummation. Love is a communion. Just as we must rediscover joy in our workplace, we can rediscover our lover.

How can we rediscover the power of pure love? We must first discover sacred love. It is not "I love you for me," but "I love you for you." We don't try to project anything, for we are happy to feel the freedom of our lover. The more he or she blooms, the happier we become for this person. When we are in altruism, in infinite love, we feel centered. Caring for our lover helps us to be more present, more intelligent, and more compassionate. The more we are present, the less we are stressed, and the happier we are.

Love can become the best teacher in our life, because to love someone requires incredible vigilance. Most of the time we are vigilant just at the beginning of the relationship for the purpose of seduction, for our ego. But once we have "won" the person, we often take them for granted.

We need to go deeper. We can feel the silence, the eternity. We can rediscover our lover every day, like the contemplation of their presence, their kindness, their humor, and their depth. When we write about a spiritual exchange missing between lovers, it does not mean that we must go to Mass every day or go to a Buddhist shrine. For some people praying together every day helps, but for others, it could have the inverse effect. Every person is special in his or her own way. Everyone comes from a special place, and we must respect the way each of us is.

In English, as in French, we use the same word to describe the love of a person and our preference for things, as when we say, "I love this salad," "I love my dog," "I love pasta," "I love to swim." But in theology, when Jesus said, "I love you," in ancient Greek, he said *agape*. What does *agape* mean? It means unconditional love beyond our projections, our needs, our seductions. In *agape*, love is not egotism, but altruism. Love is not empty, but full of grace, surprise, and happiness. We are perpetually rediscovering this kind of love. So with *agape*, we are more present. We have less stress, because the roots of our stress are not present in our lives.

Visualization: Meditate Like a Kiss

In this practice, we will learn how to be more present to our lover and how to help him or her feel more internal freedom. We will use the metaphor of the kiss. Most times, we kiss without presence. We kiss like we are brushing our teeth. But inside our bodies, a kiss activates a complex series of micro muscles and cognitive processes in our brain. To give a kiss is incredibly powerful for all of our cells.

We can meditate like a kiss anywhere, anytime, for any

person. And when we activate the kiss in our mind and on our lips, we activate a very pure and powerful energy of love inside us. A freeing energy. The goal of life is to be more alive, to be more present and more centered. We are made of love and light, so when we activate our loving energy, we recycle our fatigue.

We can meditate like a kiss for our friends and our lovers, as well as for someone we miss because of distance or who has passed away.

When we meditate like a kiss, we don't wait for reciprocation. Most of the time in surface-level life, we send love and kisses in order to have them returned. We are saddened if the person does not reciprocate. But when we practice the kiss, we are truly free because we love without any needs. We don't wait. We send a kiss, a very powerful positive energy, without reason. This is *agape*, pure altruism. We give freely. "I don't love you for me, I love you for you. And beyond that, I love you for love, for the pure energy of love."

We enter a space of incredible detachment. We become the master of our emotions. We are less stressed, more centered, and more focused.

Guidance

Exercise: Breathe All Your Love

When we send a kiss, we send our breath. But most of the time, we don't pay close attention to this moment. Our breath, our kiss, is empty and without consciousness. But we have the possibility to rediscover this incredible moment when we charge our kiss, we charge our breath, and we color this energy before we send it.

Before closing your eyes to practice, read this guidance, taking a deep breath with respect for these words.

You are sitting down,
facing your computer.
You see a picture of the person you love,
and you have decided to practice the kiss for this person.
It is an honor to practice the kiss, to send your energy.
With this practice you want to rediscover,
to reactivate your link with this person,
to reengage your love with this person.

To be together, engaged, or married is an everyday
        experience.
And every situation is an occasion to love the other person
        more deeply.

If you have some distracting thoughts, you do nothing.
You just let them pass by like clouds in the sky of your mind.

And you go back to your deep concentration, to the picture
        of your love.
Focus on this person,
see his or her face, eyes, smile.

Beyond appearances,
this person is also an energy, a soul.
In a few seconds you will be more connected to him or her.

Close your eyes.
Breathe from the bottom of your heart.
Follow the movement of your breath from heart to mind.
Feel an incredible, powerful, loving energy inside you,
a light from your heart
that you want to send to this person.

Hold your breath for three seconds,
and send your kiss
in the direction of this person.

CLOSE YOUR EYES

~

PRACTICE

~

OPEN YOUR EYES

It is amazing to be more present with a kiss, to send your love to someone every day.

Clean your mind

Diagnostic

A lot of people are fascinated by the monastic life. In the popular imagination it symbolizes the fantasy of the ultimate refuge, of pure peace. In our daily stress and difficulties, we dream of having a retreat at a monastery.

The monastic life is far from all the clichés. In Kopan, the monastery where I lived in the Himalayas, as well as in all the Carmelite convents where I stayed when I was on world tour for a play about Saint Therese—in Jerusalem, Nazareth, and Brooklyn— there is a common element that people don't see. One of the favorite activities of a monk or a nun is to clean. We clean all the time. Our cells, our kitchens, and our shrines, among other places. First, we clean out of respect. We don't live in an ordinary place, but in a sacred place, where the energy of prayer activates the energy of the monastery like a sacred fire.

But there is another reason we do it. We clean all the time because we are cleaning not only our surroundings, but also our minds. To clean our consciousness is so important. We cleanse our bodies every day. We acquire a lot of toxins on our bodies, and we enjoy taking showers to feel fresher. We feel better immediately. If we did not clean our bodies, it could be a disaster for our health.

We are vigilant with body hygiene, and yet we hardly ever clean our minds. Our emotions are like a room with socks, trousers, shoes, and shirts everywhere. Naturally, we don't like the disorder. We prefer the place to be clean and organized. Animals are also like that. This is our heritage, our ultimate nature. When our home is organized, it stimulates our brain with cognitive processes that give us the sensation and emotion of organized stability. We become calmer and our minds are clear and clean. Our ultimate nature is not to be stressed, unbalanced, and disorganized, but rather to be calm, centered, and organized. This is not a matter of dogma or morals, but of our ultimate nature.

According to spiritual traditions, the clearer our minds, the more we feel the divine energy. Each person can feel and explain the same sensation with their own words, according to their respective backgrounds, education, and cultures. We can be atheist, Buddhist, Christian, Muslim, or Jewish. We all feel the same deep sensation when all is clear, clean, and quiet in our minds. This is the reason we are so focused on this practice in monastic life. We organize our consciousness as we organize our rooms. The room is a reflection, the mirror of the mind.

In the monastic life, we train our minds night and day. We train at all times, no matter what the situation, to be more present and calm. This last practice will be conducted in movement and in action.

Visualization: Meditate Like a Broom

We will use a broom and our breath in full mindfulness to clean our minds. In the same way that we use a broom in our homes, we can visualize cleaning our mental toxins and our emotional ups and downs. For example, we can visualize our fears under our bed. When the broom gathers the dirt, we visualize that we breathe in our fears, then dispose of them while exhaling, removing them from our consciousness. Another example is when we are troubled by doubts. We can visualize those under a table. When we use the broom, we can breathe in and visualize gathering up our doubts in a pile and removing them from the floor.

We can do this with any of our emotional perturbations and addictions, all pictured in the corner of our room. We don't need to think about the reason behind the addictions, we just need to use our broom and see mentally that our negative emotions and addictions are gathered up and disposed of.

At the end, we close our eyes, we breathe deeply, hold our breath, and then picture getting rid of the dirt and dust. We dump our bad emotions, stress, anxiety, fears, and doubts into the trash.

Guidance

Exercise: Sweep Your Mind Clean

Before closing your eyes to practice, read this guidance, taking a deep breath with respect for these words.

Begin standing up,
and feel the broom in your hands.
You are connected with it.

You see the dirt under your table.

Visualize this dirt like fears hidden in your subconscious.

Start moving the broom, and at the same time, take a deep
breath.

See the movement of the emotions in your mind,

stirring from your subconscious.

Hold the breath for three seconds,

then exhale while you gather the dirt and throw it away.

Repeat the process.

Visualize your doubts, your anxiety, jealousy, violence,
addictions,

and other emotions under your bed, in a corner of your
room.

For every emotion, take a deep breath and draw the dirt
together like the broom.

Become the broom for the negative emotions hidden in your
mind

and in all the cells of your body.

Minute after minute, you see that your room is cleaner, like
your mind.

The actions of the broom in your subconscious are real.

You emotionally cleanse your home, your mind, your cells,
your organs.

You feel clearer, cleaner, calmer.

CLOSE YOUR EYES

~

PRACTICE

~

OPEN YOUR EYES

When we clean, we are completely present for our broom. It is an honor to clean. It is a blessing, an offering, a way to express gratitude. Most times, we don't truly see our life. We are too preoccupied by thoughts and distractions. We are not grateful or humble enough. When we clean our minds, we concentrate on our cleaning and not on our thoughts. We find humility.

My Path

Humility is the key to any well-being practice. Life is short, so we must focus on finding tools that genuinely help us enjoy and appreciate life instead of tools that make us look good or feed our egos.

Find Out the Lineage of the Knowledge

In the age of technology, many people act as life coaches, teaching happiness, well-being, and so forth. The best way to learn whether or not their teachings are pure is to ask where they have gained their knowledge. Most of the time, their techniques, practices, and concepts are inspired from old spiritual traditions, like Buddhism, but they have never lived in a monastery. They may have spent a couple of weeks visiting a monastery, but this is *very* different from living in one. If the source of the knowledge is not pure enough, the practice will not be powerful enough.

Many of today's teachers of well-being have learned from other happiness coaches who have learned from other coaches, whose training we don't know. You can see the pattern; the transmission from teacher to student is not pure. Part of the mastery, the intensity of the teaching, is lost. When you look beyond the surface, many of these teachers do not practice what they preach. I have taught several yoga teachers, and their biggest challenges are often stress about money problems, pressure to keep the lease at their yoga center, promotions for new customers, competition from new studios, and so forth. When the teacher's mind is not clear, the student does not receive pure teaching. When the teacher is stressed, the student mimics the teacher, and stress becomes part of their teaching habits as well. It's simply contagious.

Just as someone who has earned a PhD refers to the name of his accrediting university, a spiritual teacher must share the lineage of his masters. This information is fundamental, especially in Buddhism and all the ancient traditions. For example, an authentic Navajo medicine man gives the name of his grandfather who taught him the traditions of the tribe. In Christianity, we give the name of our congregation (Jesuit, Carmelite, and so on) and the theology we've learned through written texts.

When I teach or train teachers certified in my meditation techniques, I insist that they learn the lineage of my teachings, going back hundreds of years. In Buddhism, we have a *rinpoche* (pronounced *rin-po-shay*), a spiritual father and protector to whom we have been connected for many lives. Chepa Dorje Rinpoche was my rinpoche. He is a very special case in the tradition of Buddhism. He is the last descendant of Marpa, the translator of the Buddha Siddhartha. Further, he was the first disciple of Chatral Rinpoche, one of the highest yogis in this century, who died in the Himalayas in 2015 at the age of 102. Chepa Dorje was also master of Dzogchen (the practice of attaining the highest and most definitive path of the nine vehicles to liberation in Tibetan Buddhism), the official triple reincarnation of Jigmé Puntsok,

Jamyang Khyentsé Wangpo, and Trongteu Chepa Dorje. He was an example of how old Buddhist traditions are still alive today.

I had the chance to be taught in two lineages: Buddhism and Christianity. In Christianity, my master was the genius and well-known theologian Jean-Yves Leloup. He is one of the most revered specialists in sacred etymology in the world. He teaches by translating the exact words of Jesus from ancient Aramaic and ancient Greek to French, English, and numerous other languages. He has published more than sixty books about the translation, accuracy, and interpretation of the gospel.

Leloup also studied at Mount Athos, where the disciples of Saint John arrived many centuries ago. At Athos, the monks have developed the Christian tradition of meditation called Hesychia, which means "the stillness of the heart." In Christianity, we seldom learn about this tradition. This practice was created from a teaching in the original Greek gospel in which John asks Jesus, "Rabbi, how must we pray?" And Jesus replies, "*in pneumati, in aleteia*," meaning, "in deep breath, and with vigilance." This tradition of meditation uses many visualizations (mountain, ocean, and so on) and breathing exercises that are further used to call, receive, and transmit the Holy Spirit directly from Jesus at the Blessed Sacrament every day.

The Disciples of Our Own Lives

A fake or impure master will say, "If you follow my way, you will feel better, you will discover happiness and success, you will open your chakras, etc."

Every day, my rinpoche said exactly the opposite: "Move, Michel, don't follow me, I am the worst disciple of the Buddha.

Make your life, you will learn faster that way. You will learn better that way."

The authentic master does not want his student to become his disciple; rather, he wants the student to become the disciple of his or her own life, experiences, and mistakes. To learn in a classroom is helpful, but to put the practice in action is the only true way to test your understanding.

A true master does not give all the answers to your questions; they want you to discover some things on your own. After all, there will come a day when the master is not there to answer your questions, give you advice, or tell you the solution to your problem. If someone says they have all the answers, they are not the right teacher for you.

The Transmission of Energy

One of the most significant differences between a master and a teacher is the knowledge of the *phowa*. In the Tibetan language it means the transmission or the transfusion of energy, particularly from master to student. In the next chapter, I will explain the importance and power of the *phowa* in greater depth. Of the knowledge and expertise that I received from my rinpoche, 80 percent of the education was through the *phowa* (the transmission of his energy, his soul), and 20 percent was dharma (Buddhist principles and teachings).

The same is also true in Christianity. We can read and learn the gospel and sacred scriptures, but the most important experience is feeling the presence (the energy) of the Holy Spirit. This is divine energy that we can receive from The Christ, from God, and it can be conveyed through a priest or bishop. As they celebrate the mass they diffuse the divine energy to all who worship with them. Have you ever felt someone's prayers for you? This is the transmission of spiritual energy.

As you can imagine, many teachers in modern well-being do not diffuse a special energy, a divine energy, to their students, as a divine energy was never transmitted to them. It is not their fault! A student is only as good as his or her teacher. They teach techniques that can be practiced and repeated, but in the same way we learn piano or a sport, this rote learning lacks spiritual depth. To teach in spirituality is more than to teach techniques; a teacher must transmit their *phowa* in their experience with their student. It is a tradition many masters are desperately trying to keep relevant. They must be examples of what they teach, especially in a culture engulfed in stress. For these transfers to occur we must call, activate, and transmit a spiritual energy before every teaching.

For this book, *Meditation for Daily Stress,* the transmission of my energy is the most important outcome for readers.

Daily Life in a Monastery

To follow a deep spiritual path is not a fantasy, but rather a strict vigilance that brings a happiness unlike anything we've experienced. Devoting yourself to a spiritual life is far from the clichés that we have all heard about monastic life.

Every Saturday morning, the Kopan monastery in Nepal, where I lived, opens to the public. Most of the visitors, tourists from developed nations, explain their religious experiences as their past lives, reincarnations, and visions. Often they show beaded malas they have purchased and list off the names of "high masters" they've met. There is only one problem with this: in true Buddhist spirituality, sacred information is secret information. We do not talk casually about reincarnations, visions, or anything of that nature unless we are in private settings with high lamas. This is particularly important because many concepts and experiences can only be described in Tibetan. The English language is not precise enough to capture many concepts in the Buddhist tradition, as many of these principles explain realities beyond our perception, beyond our five senses.

Tourists who visit the monastery are surprised to see that monks are not chanting "om" in lotus position, but rather they are studying, cooking, cleaning, and playing outdoors. Many monks remain in the main temple for daily rituals called *puja*, but this is rarely open to visitors.

In traditional Tibetan culture meditation is used to wake up the mind and consciousness to see beyond appearances. Our *rigpa*—the deepest understanding of our lives—is found by waking up all levels of the mind.

Of course, people do not imagine how difficult it can be to live in a monastery; many monks and students enter into a very intense spiritual struggle. Beyond the quiet outward appearance, in every religion, in every place of worship, there is a spiritual fight. The more we want to be close to the light, the more we are tempted and faced with shadow. The shadow acts as a means of improving our faith and brings us closer to our beliefs. Many students find that staying in a monastery can be isolating, and the strict regimen can be difficult to adapt to. Furthermore, many students feel they "aren't getting it" or "aren't spiritual enough." It's not unusual for people to give up before reaping the rewards.

When some visitors decide to visit a monastery, it becomes

clear that they won't receive high teachings (sacred is secret). Rather, they feed their fantasies. When they return home, they spread a false perception of spiritual life. And many spiritual teachers try to teach or to reproduce this cliché in a yoga room or a spiritual center with Buddha statues, paintings, and so forth. It is the same when people go on a retreat at a center or in a beautiful landscape. They are so happy to find peace, and it is a great opportunity to help them. But when they return to their daily life, their mental habits are so engraved in the brain that the cognitive process of stressing starts over and the addiction returns. They have the retreat blues, also known as the spiritual blues. A few days later they are stressed again, so they have spent money for nothing, only benefiting their spiritual ego.

However, in a monastery, we also live in a fantasy. According to the U.S. Department of Health and Human Services, the first cause of stress is financial difficulties. All causes of stress are rooted in our fears. This is the main difference between life in a monastery and ordinary life. In a monastery all the monks' needs are paid for, usually through donations, which removes the concerns and distractions related to money problems. Their time and minds do not carry the financial burden that we face in ordinary life. In a monastery, we pray, we learn, we teach about a reality that most of the time we never see—we do not have to commute to work, or wait in traffic, or deal with the stresses most people face. It is truly a blessing, but obviously it is not realistic for everyone.

Every day, while living in the monastery, I wondered how we could bridge the gap between spiritual fantasy and spiritual reality.

This is my mission for this book, and for everyone I meet.

The Three Foundations
of Meditation: Phowa, Tonglen,
and Hesychia

The Phowa

The importance of lineage in our way of meditation

We carry with us the memories of our teachers, which Carl Jung explained as the collective unconscious. We know how it offers information far beyond our ordinary capacities. Sometimes our lives find direction because our teachers have provided love and inspiration.

The same truth applies when we are sick. The relation that we can have with our doctor is so important. If we are close to death, the hospital team is crucial.

The same is true when we love someone (a lover, our families, friends). We know how their presence is important, both at the moment of death and throughout our life. So we know how the energy between two people, the motivation of the heart, is at the center of our memories and our lives. And at the moment of our death, this is the most important support we can have. When we die, we let go of everything except the good energy of love that we have given. We never lose what we gave.

When we learn a practice or technique, the relationship with the teacher is important. In meditation, if the teacher is only technical, we feel that lack of warmth, and it is difficult to expend effort. It is the same for any discipline. For example, if your music teacher is kind and warm, you make more progress. The kinder the teacher's heart, the better you feel, and the better your practice.

With my teaching we use visualization and breath (mind and body) as in any meditation technique (yoga, MBSR, etc.), but we also enter into a lineage of knowledge, a lineage of pure energy. We are connecting with the pure source of a spiritual experience, transfused through many centuries.

In the Tibetan language, the name of this transmission of energy is *phowa*. In Vajrayàna Buddhist meditation practice, *phowa* means the "transfusion of consciousness," or "transference of our consciousness at the time of death." In this book, I focus on the transfer of energy through *phowa* and focus less on the power of *phowa* at death. If you want more information on this topic, you must meet a high lama. I am not a lama. I am just a bridge between two worlds, a translator.

How does the phowa work?
During our lifetime, there are people we love with all our hearts: our lovers, our friends, our family. The relationship we can have with our teachers is also important.

There are also some people we love beyond our hearts, because the connection comes from divine energy, like saints, our rinpoche, or our bodhisattva. There is someone unique in our life, like a guide, a primary source of inspiration. In Christianity, it is the same. We have a favorite saint, or it can be the Virgin Mary, or Jesus. So during our life, day after day, we have developed and fed our relationship through our prayers and our offerings to this saint, to this special energy. He or she is familiar to us. Through our saint, our bodhisattva, we receive signs or synchronicities. We are confident in our guide. At the moment of death, as at birth, we are so fragile. We need to be supported, and our saint will be there.

When we drink a glass of water, we can feel, smell, and see the provenance of the water. When we swallow the water, we can feel the journey of the source (the rain, the clouds, the sky) of this water in our body. To be present to a simple glass of water is a form of *phowa*. The water transfers its energy, just as a rinpoche transfers his energy to our hearts, to our souls, and to every cell in our bodies.

The *phowa* is one of the cornerstones of this way of meditation. It is more than a way to feel less stress; it enables us to feel better immediately because we are connected to a pure, positive energy.

My spiritual intuition to adapt meditation for emergency situations involving daily stress was to adapt *phowa* for the workplace. When I teach, I reactivate my rinpoche's energy inside me, and I send this special energy and inspiration to everyone I teach. The moment I begin to guide visualization, I see and send a ray of light to everyone in the room.

This form of meditation is 20 percent visualization and 80 percent *phowa*.

When I am not physically present, I send this energy via Skype. I have discovered that it works through a screen, on a video, or in an application, because energy moves through any material support. When you read this book, you receive the energy I transmit through my words, with all of the lineage behind my teachings.

Tonglen

The original sense of tonglen: to recycle

My way of meditation finds one of its roots in the Tibetan concept of *tonglen*. The word means "to give and to receive." We can translate this as "to recycle." For me it was a revelation when I discovered this concept, especially in the modern world, where stress is contagious. The answer is not to say that the world is so stressful, but to ask what can we do with this stress? How can we use the energy of stress and transform or recycle it? How can we adapt the concept of *tonglen* to the modern world?

I first heard about *tonglen* fifteen years ago from my friend Dr. Amchi Tsetan. I was so sick in my stomach, so stressed, like billions of people are. For me, stress was normal, because every person around me was stressed. I had seen many doctors in France for my stomach, and they explained to me that I must go to the hospital for surgery. The prognosis was critical. When I saw Dr. Tsetan, he explained that the pain, the energy of the stress, had chosen to stay in my stomach with acidity. He gave me Tibetan medicine, and he explained the Tibetan concept of *tonglen*. He explained that the root of my sickness was that I was keeping bad emotions inside of me. Just the idea of recycling, of letting go of these emotions, was a game changer.

So with Tibetan medicine and a lot of *tonglen* visualizations to recycle stress, I was totally cured. The French doctors were amazed.

In every practice of this book, *tonglen* is present. There are many visualizations, mental pictures, and breath exercises to learn how to recycle. *Tonglen* is more than detoxing; it is recycling, changing darkness to light, transforming the suffering that we receive into positive energy that we share with our bodies, our coworkers, our friends, our families, and our surroundings.

The mental toxins we breathe in have become one of the most dangerous pollutants both to our planet and to our interior cosmos. As science shows, everything is energy, and energy cannot be destroyed; it can merely be transformed. When a billion people create a billion tons of mental toxins and suffering at every second, we breathe in and diffuse this mental and spiritual pollution.

We can compare mental pollution to plastic pollution in the natural environment. Plastic pollution destroys our ecosystem and our planet. Mental pollution destroys our bodies and our consciousness.

The difference between physical pollution and stress pollution is like the difference between the visible and the invisible.

It is easy to see plastic pollution; it is material and therefore visible. But stress, which is mental pollution, is invisible. Because we cannot see it physically as a pollutant, we just live with it. Compounding the issue, we are not educated in identifying and understanding mental toxins. Education is key. But no political leader, and few spiritual leaders, are interested in this form of pollution, which is probably the most toxic on our planet.

To minimize plastic pollution, we have learned to take some precautions. We take reusable bags to the supermarket, and some places have banned the use of plastic bags. We have created companies and systems to recycle plastic pollutants.

But for stress, for mental pollution, we learn nothing. No one explains to us how mental toxins are dangerous and contagious. We are not educated enough to know that we should recycle these toxins, and we wouldn't know how to recycle them even if we wanted to. But just as we recycle plastic, we have the capacity to recycle these mental pollutants that kill us year after year. Stress is compounded by ignorance.

There are two steps to learning how to recycle our stress.

1. Detox. In the practices in this book, we develop the skills of detoxification. We learn to exhale the negative energy we receive so we no longer keep it inside us or around us.

For this, we use very powerful visualizations that contain a metaphor, or a symbol, such as meditating like a wave or like a dolphin. We also use breathing exercises; we learn how to inhale, to hold our breath, and then to exhale as we mentally see the dark energy exiting our minds and our cells.

2. *Transform.* After learning breath work, we add visualizations that focus on transforming darkness to light.

Why is recycling mental toxins so easy? It is because the act of recycling is something that we do every single day. We breathe in, hold our breath, and exhale. Without knowing it, every person in the world practices *tonglen* naturally, but most of the time, we do not pay attention to our breath. It is human nature to recycle, to rid ourselves of the bad energies within us.

The goal of *tonglen* is not to learn something new, but to rediscover how we can use what we naturally do to avoid being sad, anxious, or stressed.

Through *tonglen* we understand that our ultimate nature is to recycle and to be at peace. To recycle is our nature; it is no coincidence that when we eat, we then go to the restroom. It is the same process. We take in, we keep, and then we expel. Nothing is more natural or easier to practice than *tonglen*.

When we are in a state of having forgotten our nature, we are in a state of death. When we reactivate our natural mechanism, we are more alive. In every practice of this book, the goal of *tonglen* is to see how easy and effortless it is to meditate, and how immediately the effects occur, because to recycle is our nature.

It is not new.

But it has been forgotten.

Hesychia and Hesychasm

Hesychasm, which refers to the stillness or peace of the heart, is a very old Eastern Orthodox Christian tradition that teaches us to be calmer. It is based on Christ's injunction in the Gospel of Matthew that "when thou prayest, enter into thy closet, and when thou hast shut thy door, pray." Traditionally, Hesychasm has been the process of retiring inward by ceasing to register the senses, to achieve an experiential knowledge of God. When we are in Hesychia, we are in a state of peace independent of external circumstances.

After the time of Jesus, when John came to Patmos, Greece, with his disciples, he may have started to work on this type of prayer. Most likely, with his disciples, John meditated on the teaching from Jesus. Then the disciples went to Mount Athos. There, monks developed Hesychia. This practice, which uses visualization and breath exercise to achieve internal peace, spread from monk to monk down a pure lineage for many centuries. As a result, Mount Athos became famous for the tradition of Hesychia.

I have received this teaching from Jean-Yves Leloup, my wonderful spiritual master. Jean-Yves was a monk, a hermit at Mount Athos. He has received transmission of this tradition from Father Seraphin, who was the disciple of Saint Silouane, and so forth. This lineage comes straight from the story of Saint John, most beloved disciple of Jesus.

Jesus said to his disciples, "Peace, I leave you, my peace I give you." Jesus was teaching us a quality of peace not based on our temporary, fleeting world. He was teaching us instead a deep and freeing peace, independent of exterior circumstances.

This is why I adopt and teach the genius visualization of the monks. Hesyschia uses mental pictures like a mountain, an ocean, a sunflower, and so on, as well as postures, which are exercises with breath.

Through this method of meditation, you will discover how your problems can become your spiritual teacher. You will discover how to love your problems and how your traumas and addictions can become the highest teaching in your life. If you want to work with less stress, to be more intuitive, creative, and loving, the first step is to achieve a quiet mind, like a pure lake or a pure sky. You must develop a quality of calm that you can practice freely, anytime and anywhere. Why is that possible, and even easy? Because it is our nature. We are born from peace, and we go to eternity. Peace is everywhere, like oxygen. Life is simple. Peace is simple. Love is simple. God is simple. We are complicated for no reason, for ego, out of ignorance. So yes, we can be at peace, the quality of peace that Jesus gave to his disciples.

Acknowledgments

Special thanks to Chelsea Cooper for adapting this manuscript for publication in English. Thanks also to my family: Louis, Jocelyn, and Lyndsey Cooper, and Ms. Susy and Ms. Buttercup Cooper.

Thanks to Silouane Pascal, Christophe Pascal, Marie-José Pascal, and Marilia and Antonia Cracchiolo.

I am deeply grateful to my agents, Johanna Maaghul and Bill Gladstone, to Dr. Mario Beauregard and Dr. Natalie Trent, and to my publisher, Abrams. At Abrams thanks go to Michael Sand, Garrett McGrath, Annalea Manalili, and Darilyn Carnes.

Thank you to Yasmin Molazadeh and my friends at Google, Bayard Russell, Tamara Stern, Yuliia Zabiyaka, and Van Rippen.

To Sylvie Brousseau and Debie Gilman at Park La Brea, Los Angeles, my sincere gratitude.

Thank you also to Mark Faucette and to my friends at Amity Foundation.

For their kindness and wisdom, my thanks to Jean-Yves Leloup, Tulku Chepa Dorje Rinpoche, Claude Dordis, Amchi Tsetan, Juliana Klinkert, Monseigneur Guy Sansaricq, Pere Borno, Maître Denis Blouin, Laurent Robin, David Klein, Blaise Kremer, Katherine Blair, Abigael Martinez, Jonathan Dimmock, Frank Brownstead, Louie Gooey, Siberia Su, Mayra Pool, Karen Keller, Lana Moyzuk, Feliz Salas, Laurent Stopnicki and Carole Serrat, and Gabriella Wright.

Special thanks to the legendary yoga master Sri Dharma Mittra; to Andrew Jones and Pam, Adam Frei, Johanna, and the whole team at Dharma Yoga Center of New York; to my producer Andrea Correa and to Maria Isabella Correa. And, finally, thank you to Tonya Jacobs and her team at the Mercedes Club New York.

About the Author

Michel Pascal is a French writer, meditation teacher, singer, photographer, composer, and director of spiritual documentaries. Before moving to the United States, Pascal lived in the Kopan Monastery in Nepal. The high master Chepa Dorje Rinpoche (a descendant of Marpa) was his meditation teacher for fifteen years. Pascal has also studied Christian theology under Jean-Yves Leloup and has written sixteen books in French about spirituality.

Pascal has taught at the Dharma Yoga Center in New York City and at the Amity Foundation in Los Angeles. He has given workshops at Harvard University and at the corporate offices of Google. His solo musical show, "Relax-Sing," was performed at Carnegie Hall in November 2016. With the Amity Foundation, Pascal is creating the first meditation program for the neediest people in America.

Pascal invites you to follow his teachings, practices, and documentaries on michelpascal.tv or on Twitter @michelmeditates.

Editor: Michael Sand
Designer: Darilyn Lowe Carnes
Production Manager: Alex Cameron

Library of Congress Control Number: 2016949533

ISBN: 978-1-4197-2405-3

Text copyright © 2017 Michel Pascal
Illustrations copyright © 2017 Maria Isabel Correa

Printed and bound in the USA
10 9 8 7 6 5 4 3 2 1

Abrams Image books are available at special discounts when purchased in
quantity for premiums and promotions as well as fundraising or educational
use. Special editions can also be created to specification. For details,
contact specialsales@abramsbooks.com or the address below.

ABRAMS The Art of Books
115 West 18th Street, New York, NY 10011
abramsbooks.com